בכל דור ודור עומדים עלינו לכלותנו

In every generation they rise up against us to destroy us

Adapted from the Haggadah (c. ninth–tenth century CE), a testament to the trials of each generation and a reminder that we have endured, we have remained, and we have carried hope forward.

Ashkenazi
Beta Israel
Chabad-Lubavitch
Conservadox
Conservative
Crypto
Cultural
Haredi
Hasidic
Humanistic
Jew by Choice
Jew(ish)
Liberal
Mizrahi
Modern Orthodox
Orthodox
Post-Denominational
Progressive
Reconstructionist
Reform
Renewal
Satmar
Secular
Sephardic
Ultra-Orthodox
Unaffiliated

Just Jewish

I recognize there's probably no two Jews in the world who will agree on what it means to be Jewish.

I don't follow all the Jewish laws, but I do follow some of them.

I do not consider myself as identifying with any of the religious denominations of Judaism. I would consider myself just Jewish.

Well, at the bones level, I'm the child of Jewish parents.

I'm Jewish partly from a religious perspective, but more so from a cultural and tradition perspective.

We call ourselves Conservadox. So I wouldn't say I'm full-blown Orthodox.

Well, it's meant different things at different times in my life, that's for sure. I had a pretty religious upbringing.

The grandparents were ultra-Orthodox; my parents less so.

For me, Judaism is a religion and it's a culture and it's an ethnicity. I would argue it's perhaps even a nationality to me—though that could be controversial.

I'm Jewish on both sides, but different style Jews. I've always felt a little bit of racism from both sides. You don't think about it—you think all Jews are one kind, but they're really not. My dad was from Iraq. He was born in Baghdad and left when he was fourteen or fifteen. He doesn't have proper records as a lot of people who are refugees do not.

My mom's side of the family were Ashkenazi Jews from Wales. For me, it's more of a cultural thing, because I don't consider myself a religious person. It's my culture. In a way they are my people.

I didn't grow up with any Jews. I find that as I grow older, and the less time I spend in Jewish spaces, the more Jewish I tend to be.

I think it's an opportunity to belong to organized Jewish life, and I enjoy belonging. I enjoy meeting people with whom I have a profound commonality. It's in some ways undefinable, but it's there. It can't be coherently explained, no matter how many words you use.

I would say it's being part of something that's bigger than yourself—a community that's bigger than you and that will always be there for you.

It is so much more than just a religion, or so much more than just a culture. It's kind of this global community. There's something that unites us all; we have this common bond that keeps us together.

Because Jews were excluded from so much it forced them to be closer and have a greater bond and togetherness, because they were all in it themselves. Not against everybody else, but everybody seemed to be against them. The only thing they could do as Jews was to bind themselves together. And that meant closer connections between themselves, whether it was friendship level, business level, or educational level, and self-help societies where they tried to help each other out. I think Jews were able to succeed in the face of all the adversity because they had their own community to make themselves better.

It's hard for me to relate to the religious/observant Judaism. It's hard to feel when, as a trans person, I know how not accepting a lot of physical Jewish spaces are.

Some people have a traditional image of what a Jewish person looks like, and I don't always fit into a category. I would get a lot of interesting questions like, "Are you an Ethiopian Jew?" or "Is that just for decoration?" or "Did your girlfriend give you that?"

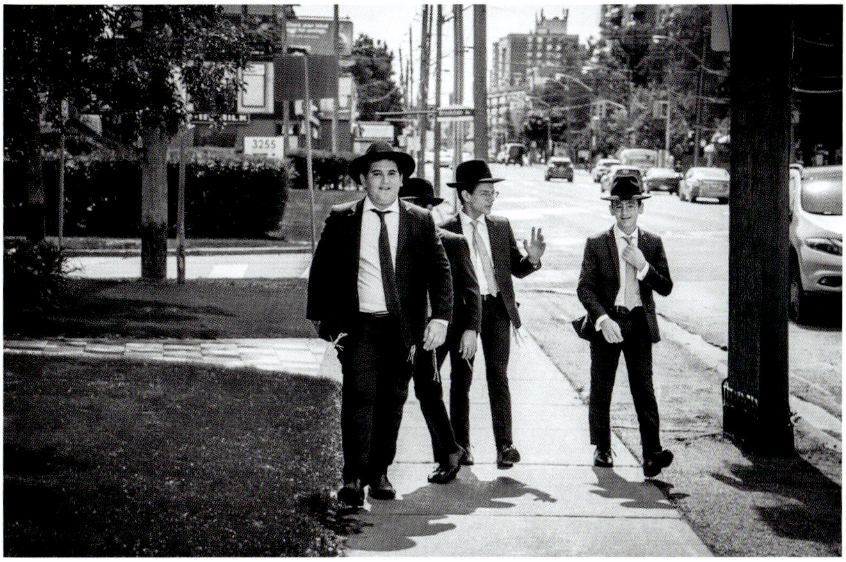
3255

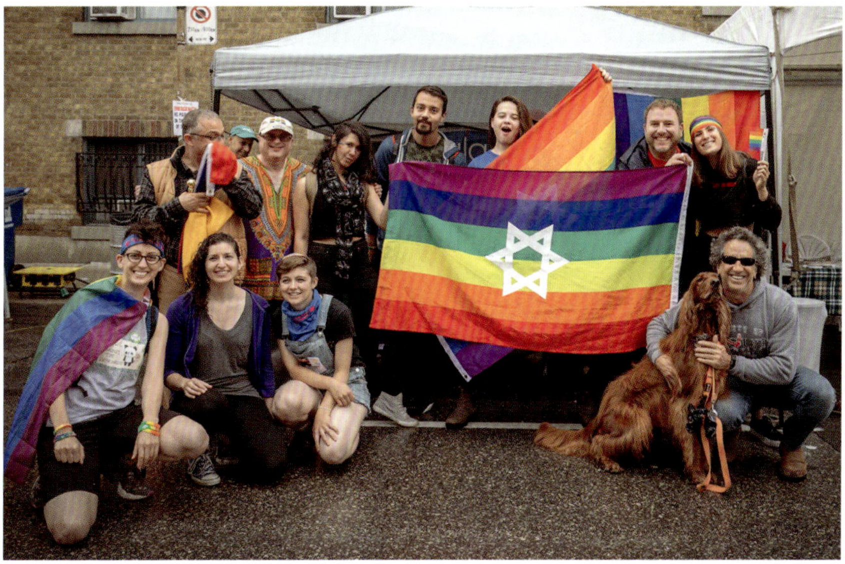

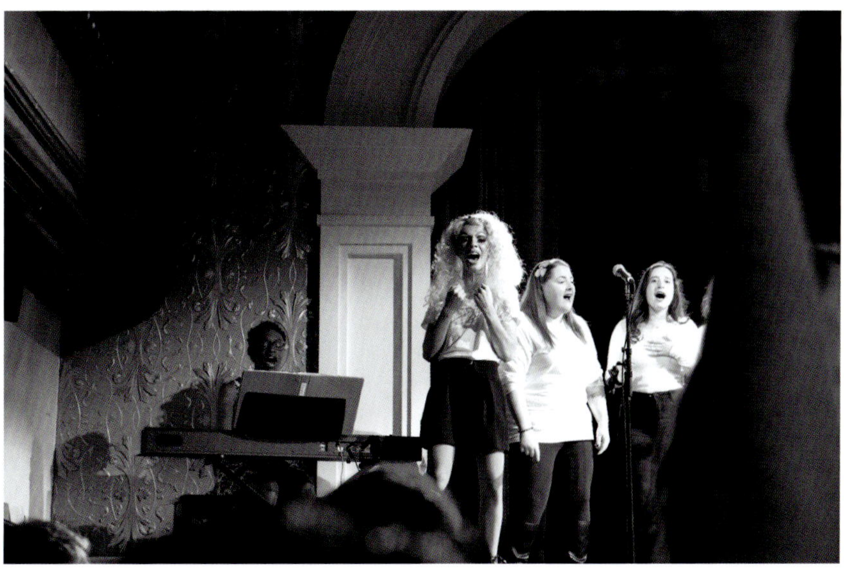

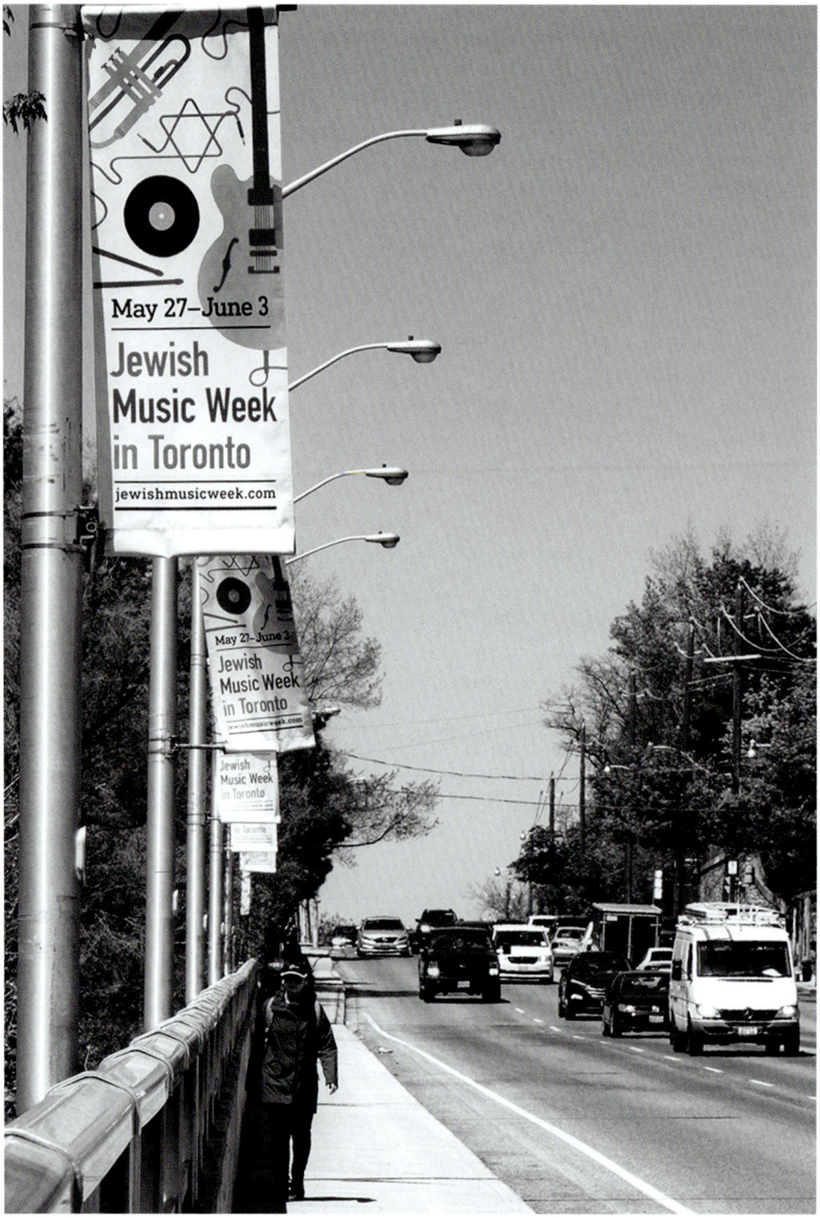
May 27–June 3
Jewish
Music Week
in Toronto
jewishmusicweek.com

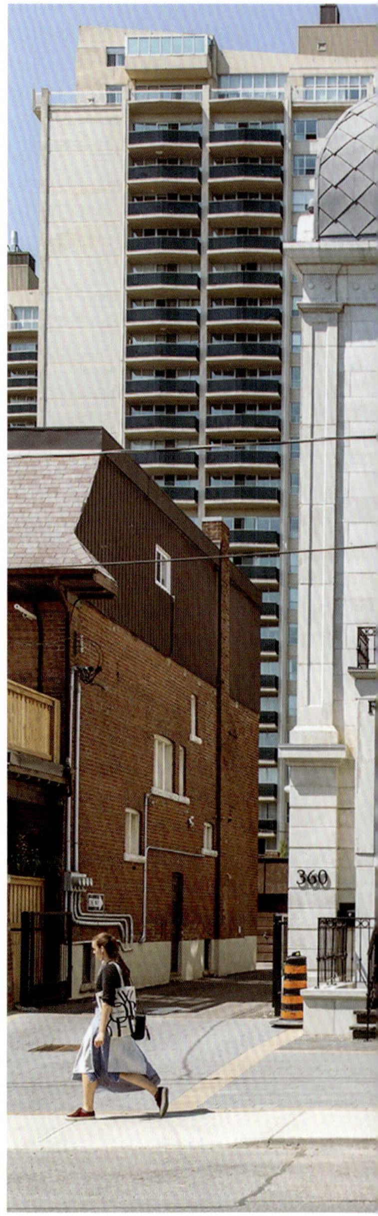
360

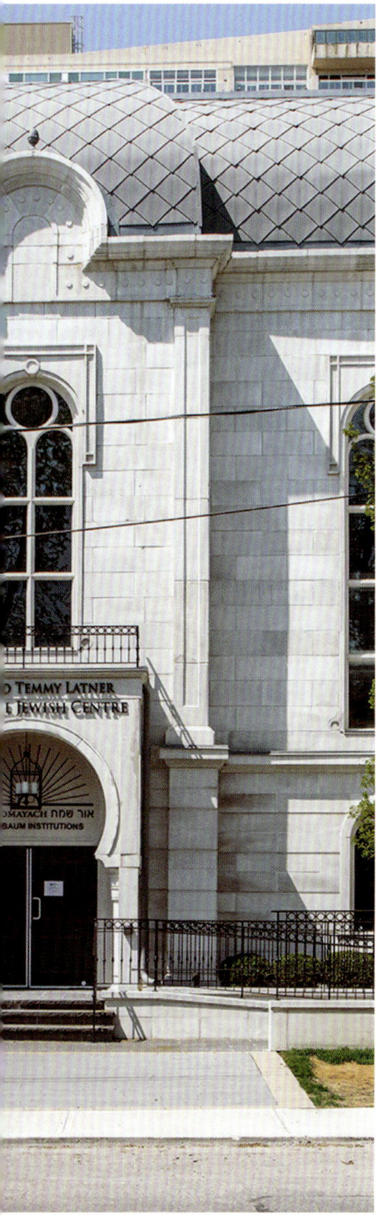
TEMMY LATNER
JEWISH CENTRE
OMAYACH אור שמח
BAUM INSTITUTIONS

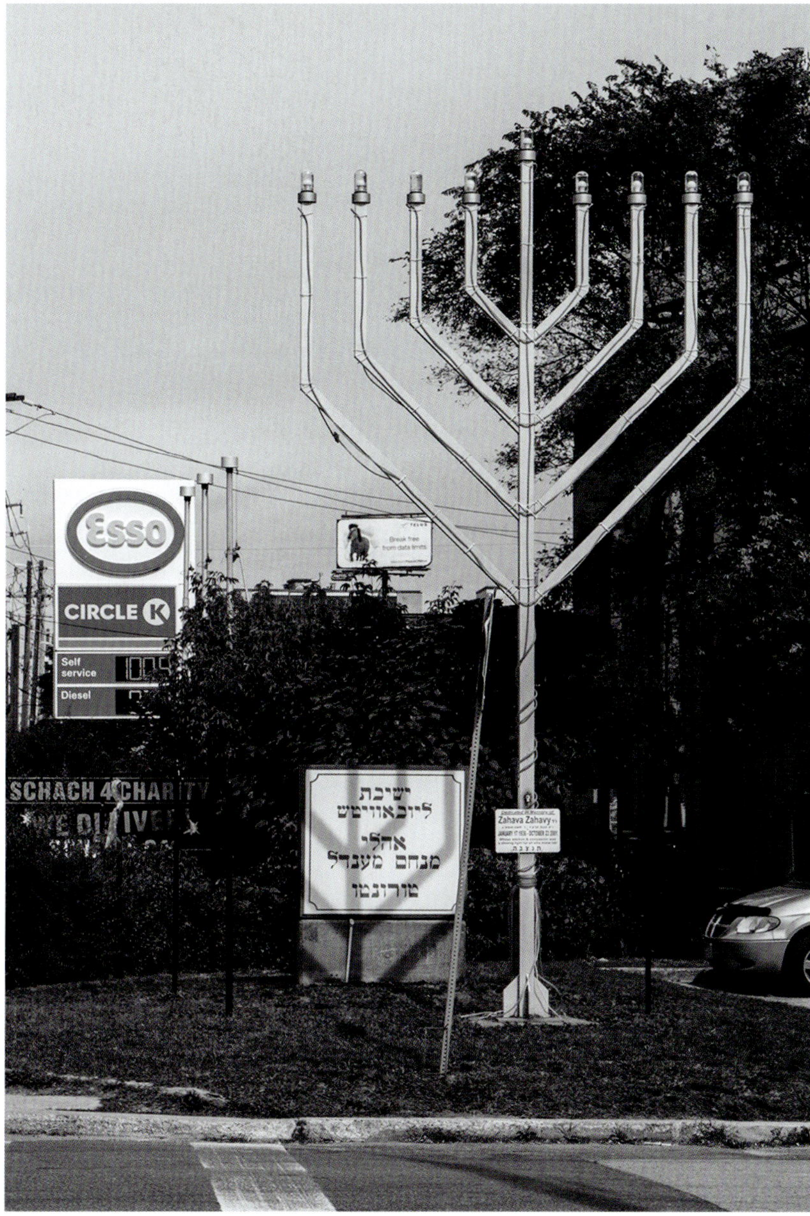
Esso
CIRCLE K
Self service
Diesel
SCHACH 4 CHARITY
ישיבת
ליובאוויטש
אהלי
מנחם מענדל
טורנטו
Zahava Zahavy

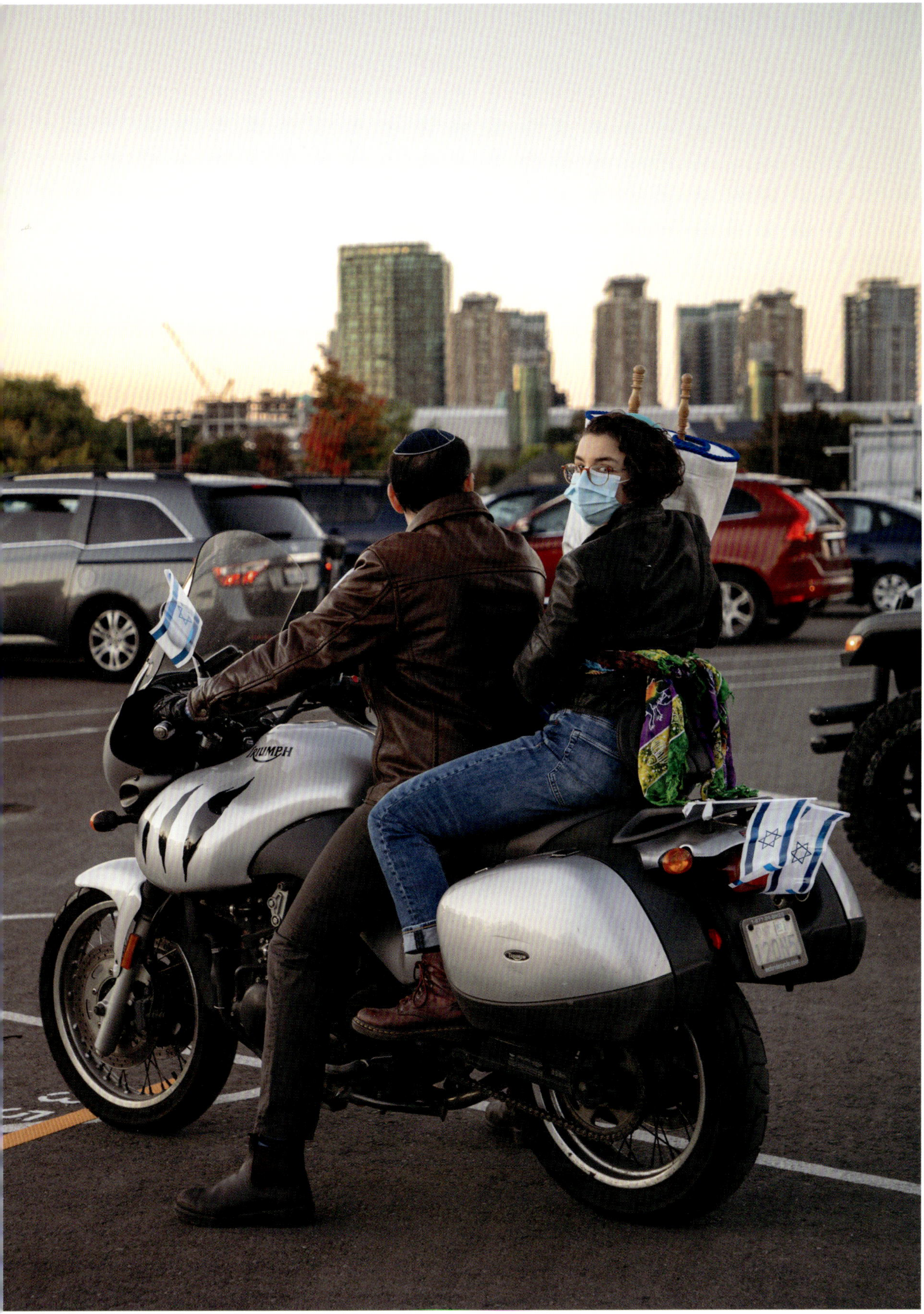
TRIUMPH

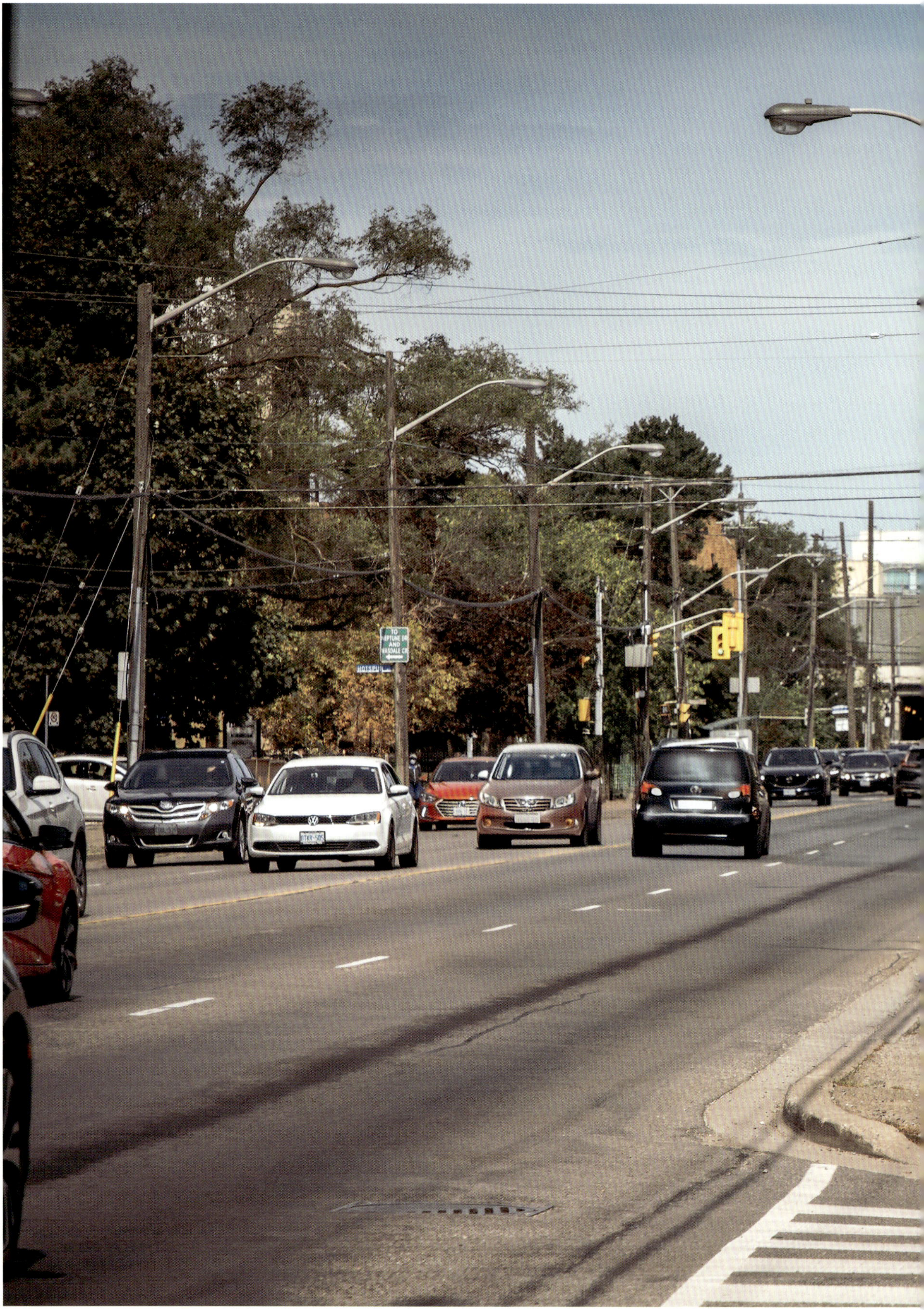
TO
AND

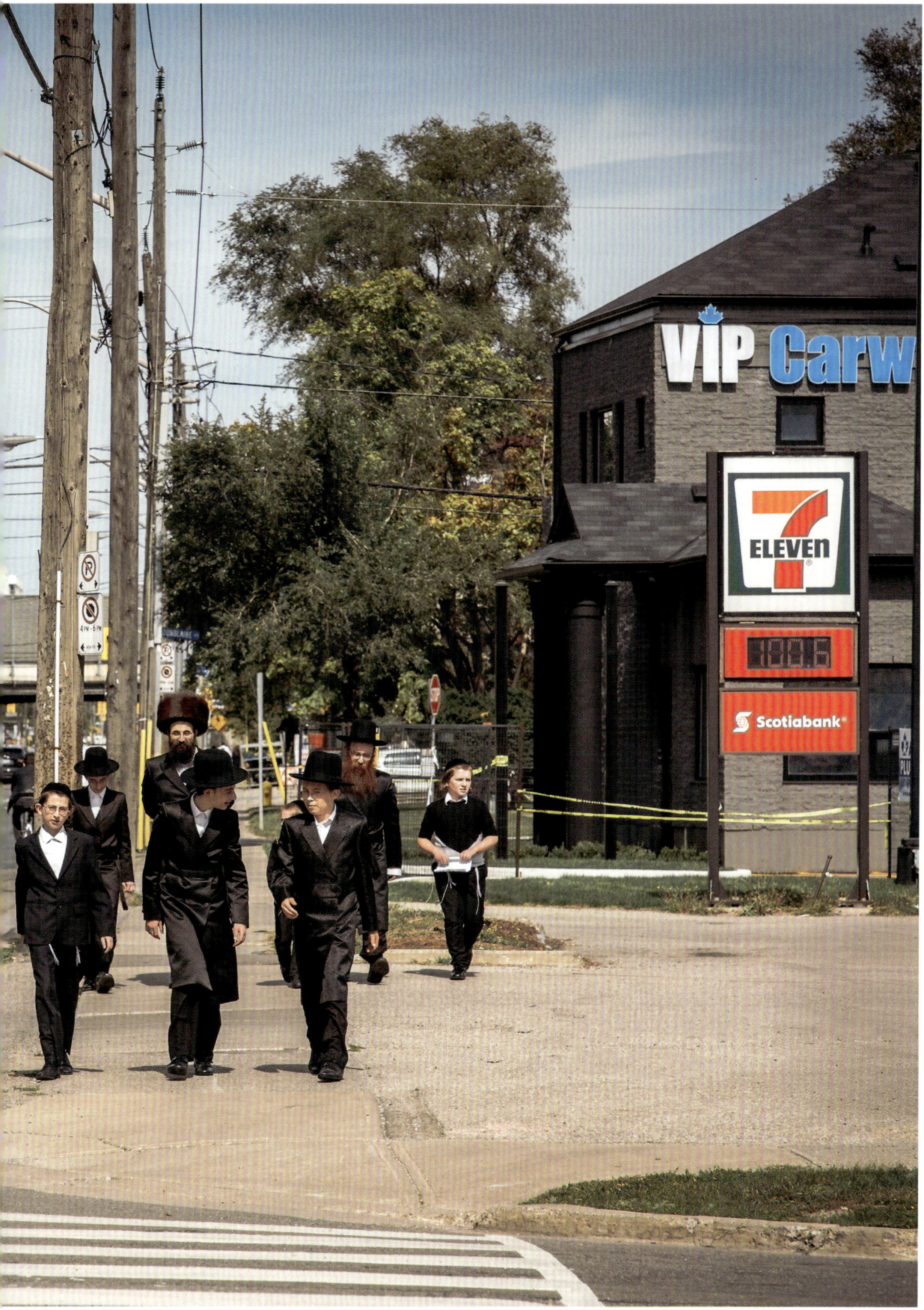
VIP Carw
7 ELEVEN
Scotiabank

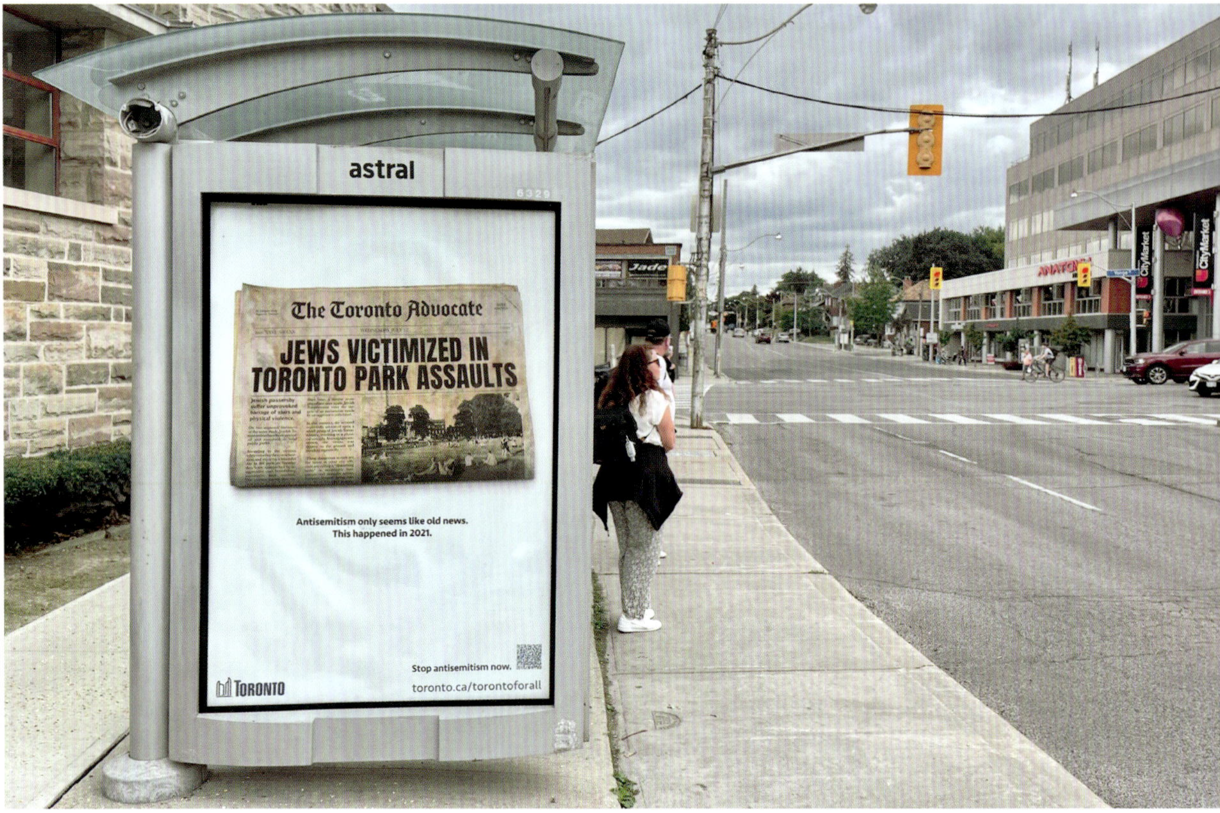
astral
6329
The Toronto Advocate
JEWS VICTIMIZED IN TORONTO PARK ASSAULTS
Antisemitism only seems like old news.
This happened in 2021.
Stop antisemitism now.
toronto.ca/torontoforall
TORONTO
Jade
CityMarket

I feel more threatened, even though I haven't encountered antisemitism.

It still seems way over there, which I think is a dangerous way to think about it because it's not way over there. It just hasn't landed here yet.

When I hear those things, it frightens me. I find it so hard to understand, in this day and age, that there's antisemitism. It's traveled the world; there's just no safety for Jews anymore. And that's very frightening.

I find the rise of antisemitism threatening as a Jew, even in North America where our rights are enshrined.

This is happening not too far away. This is happening in our neighborhoods, in our communities. It's not just happening in Europe.

Why it is that a very high percentage of the incidents are against Jews in a city like Toronto, which is supposedly so open and so diverse?

I'm not counting on people at this stage of my life. I read about antisemitism, and if it becomes wider spread, then it could have a possible effect on our offspring.

The impact is not necessarily for myself, but for my kids and my grandkids.

There are individuals my age who are saying antisemitic things or doing antisemitic actions. That surprises me, because from my perspective, for our generation, that should be a thing of the past. We should be better than that, but obviously we are not.

I was washing my hands and there were three guys that were not Jewish making comments about me and my Jewish friends, and they were threatening comments. I remember I was surprised because I thought we were friends.

Open antisemitism is a worrisome development. Jews have always been hated by the right wing. Always—no surprise there, put them aside. So the news is really in the left wing.

The impact of what takes place in other countries makes it easier for antisemitism to grow in a country like Canada. That's what I feel is taking place.

I was a student at York University, and I was a student at University of Toronto. In both environments there was a substantial amount of antisemitic activity.

I do have quite a Jewish last name, which I think is something to always kind of have an eye out about because I can't hide that.

Uber's a good example. I don't think if I was in an Uber with my friends that we would talk about being Jewish.

I would say the biggest shock for me was when there was the white-supremacist rally in Charlottesville a few years ago and there were young dudes walking through the streets saying, "Jews will not replace us." That was like a huge wake-up call of like, holy shit, these people really want to kill Jews.

I'm Black, and so people would just say I'm Black before anything else. And for Jews that are also White, I think a lot of them feel, "I'm Jewish, I'm not White."

One of the questions was, What do I consider my race or ethnicity? There was a list of options, and I had to check off the box—it was White, Caucasian, Black, Asian, etc., you know, those kinds of options. I sat on that question for at least half an hour, and I got really frustrated. As a Jewish person, yes, I'm White passing, but for me, I don't identify with people who are White, because when my grandparents were living in Europe—and they were Jewish—there were the Poles and there were the Jews, and they were not the same people. It wasn't like the Jews were White; they were never considered White.

I don’t feel any connection to Polish or Austrian culture in the slightest, but I do feel a strong connection to Jewish culture through those same family members. Their nationality is not important to me, but their cultural identity has been important to me.

I think about how my dad had to suffer so much being Jewish, and how my families have moved because of the pogroms in Latvia and Iraq.

My grandmother talked about it, whereas my grandfather didn’t. She got to work in the kitchen in Auschwitz, whereas my grandfather was in the slave camps.

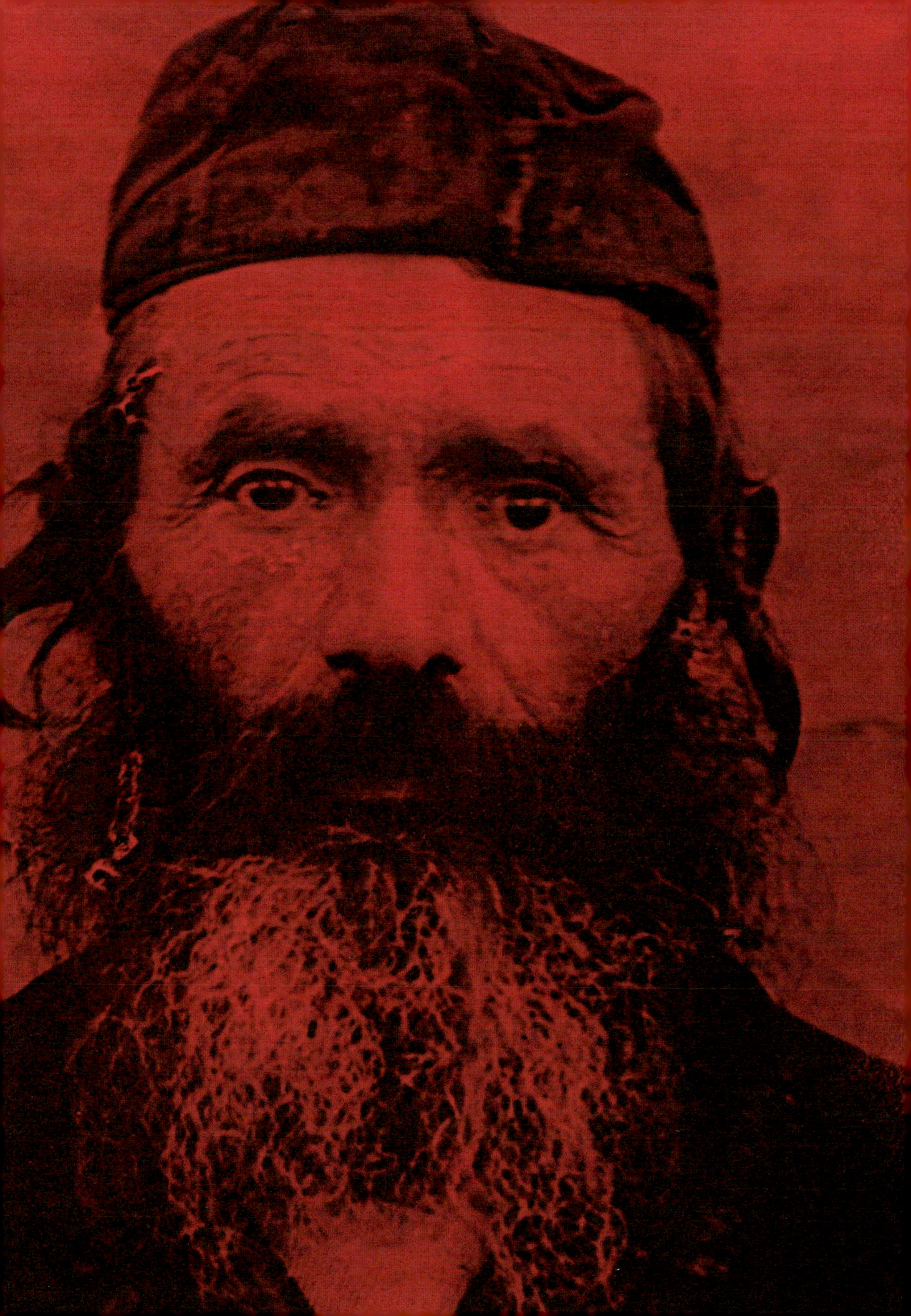

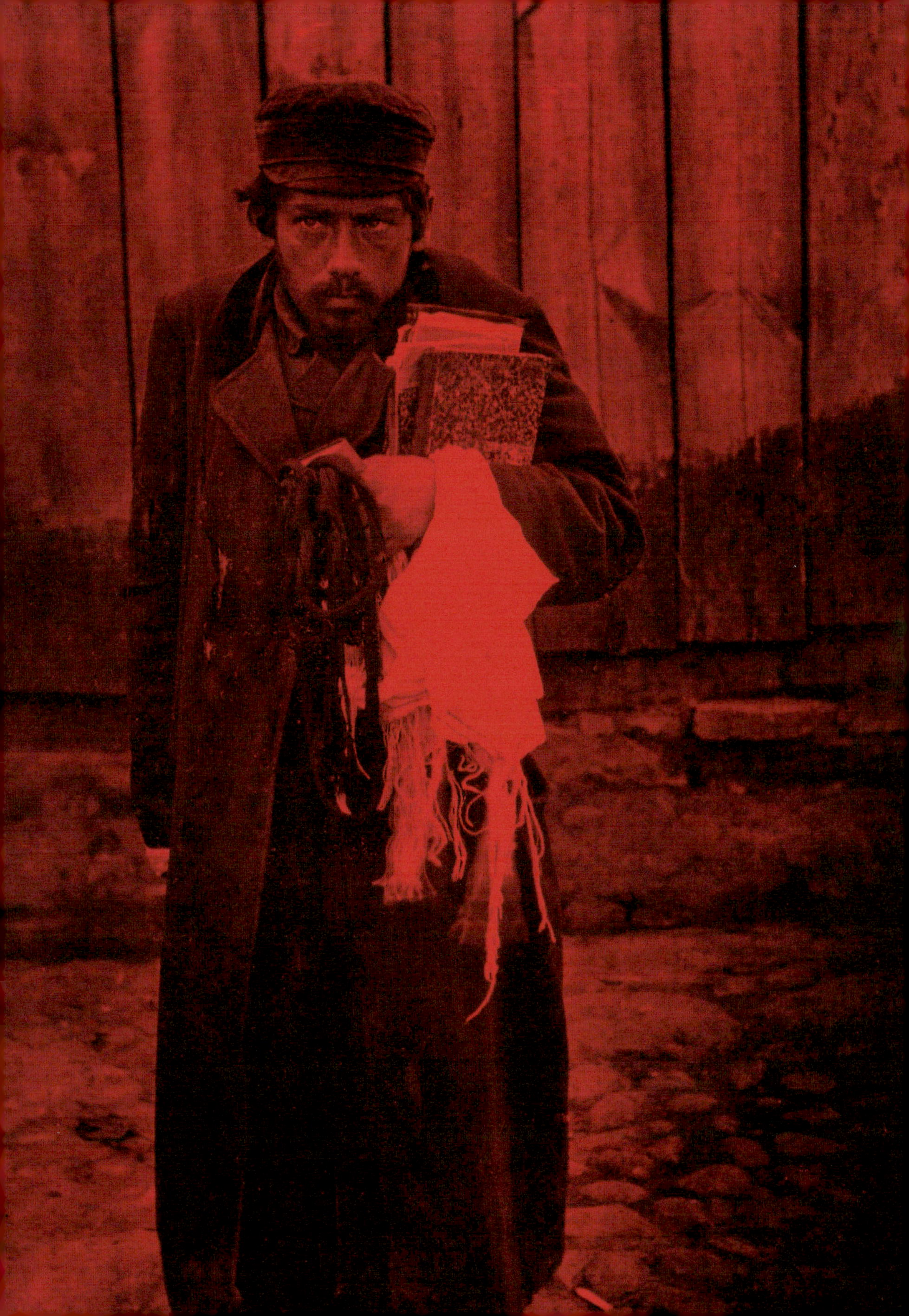

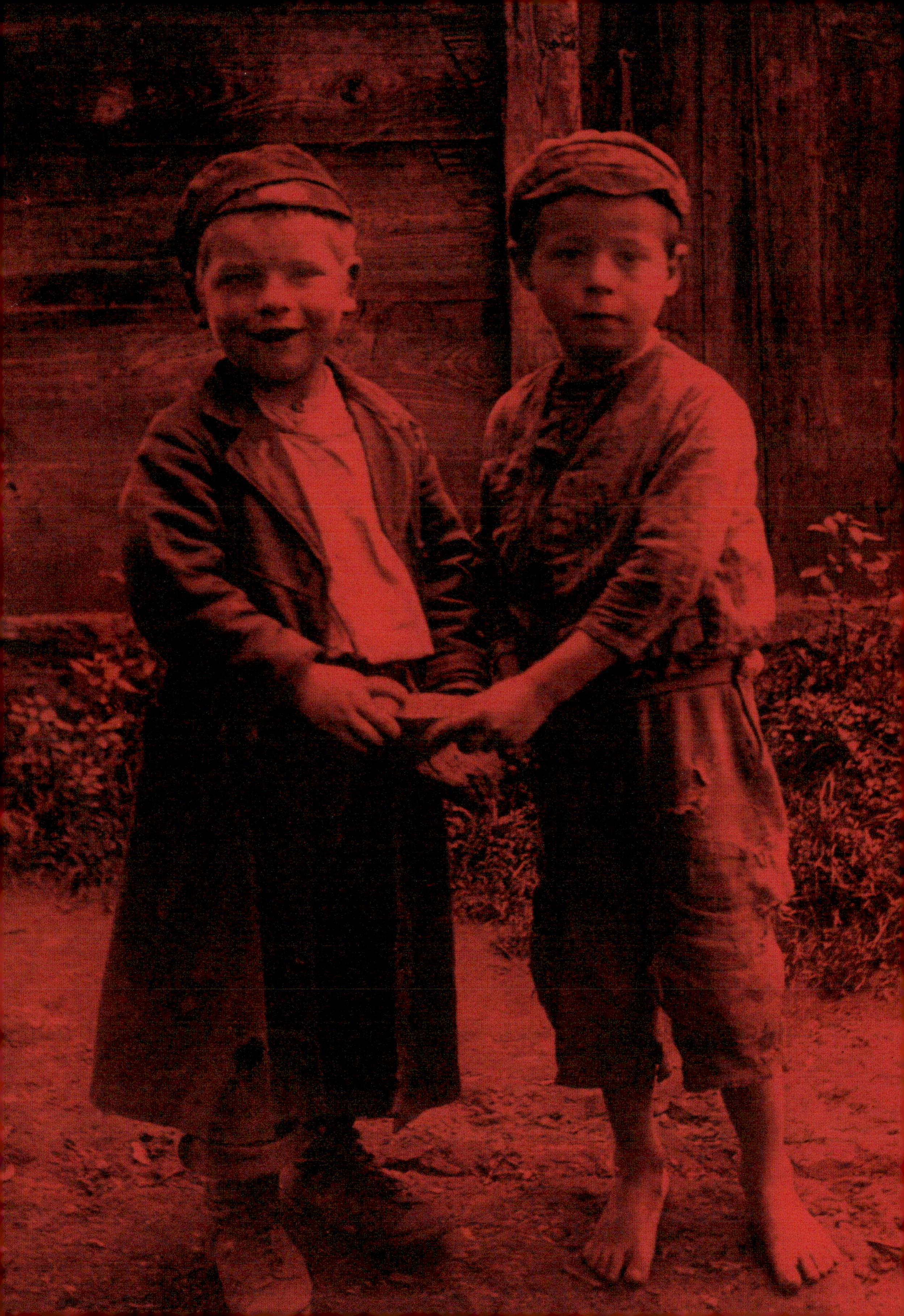

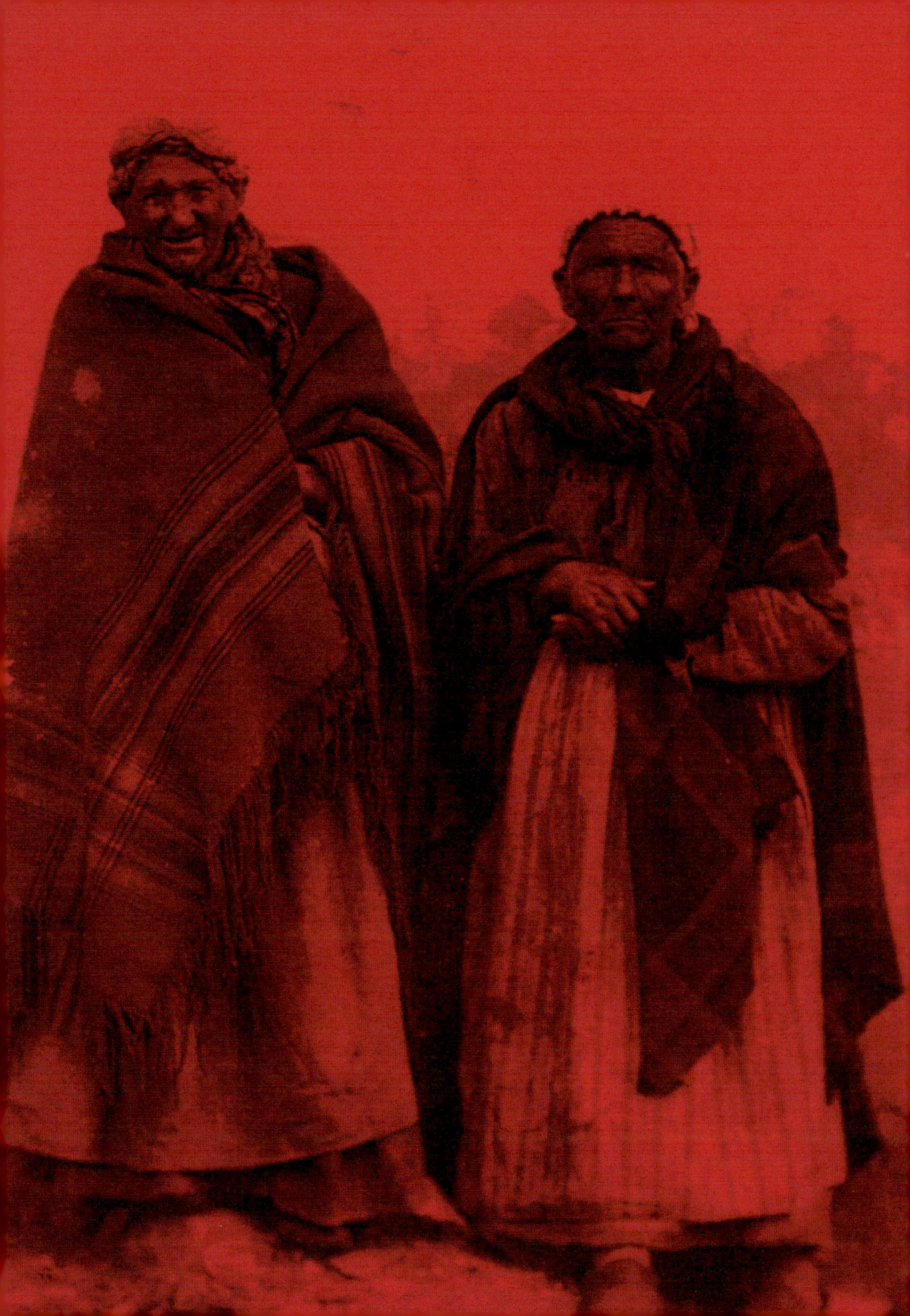

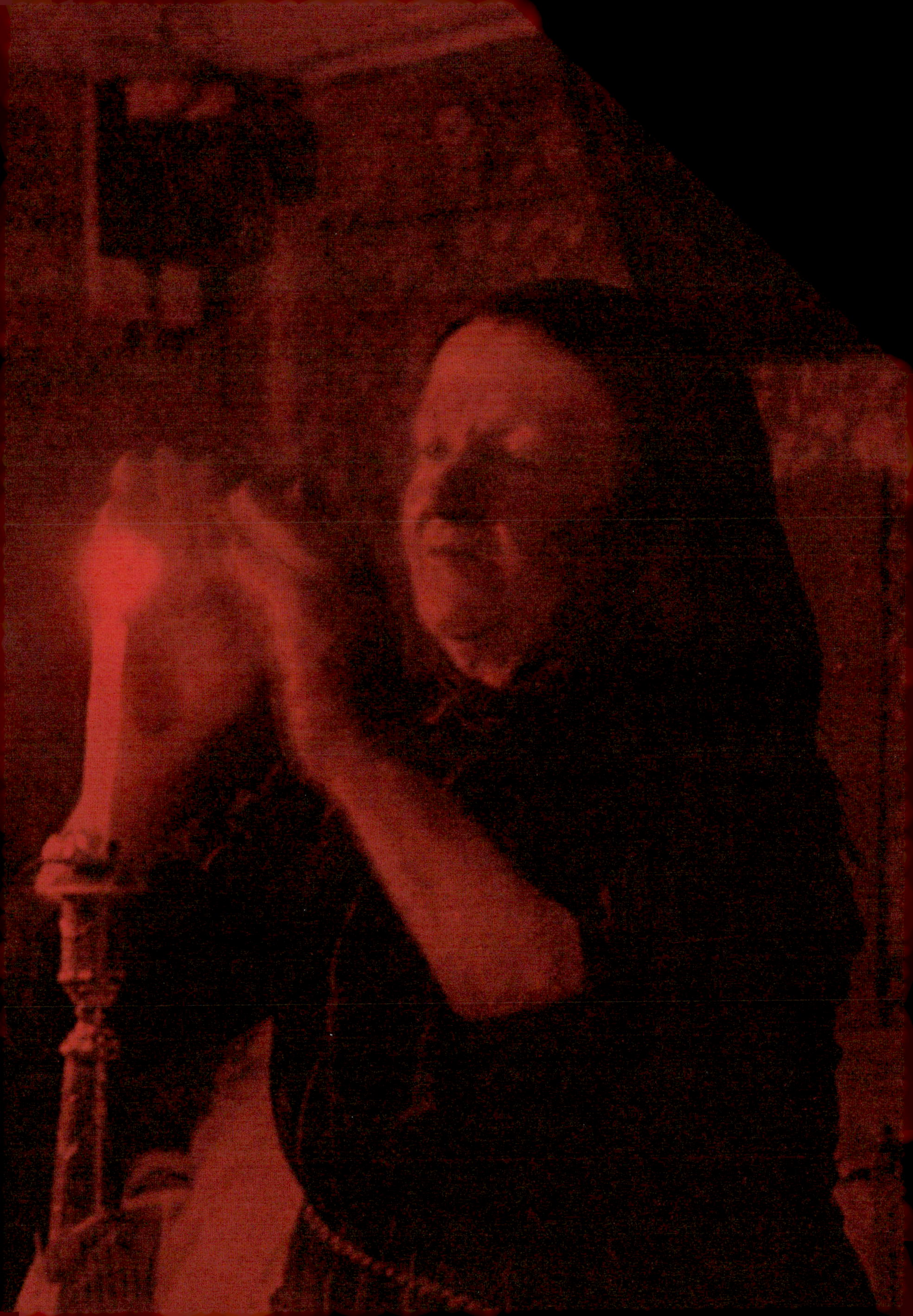

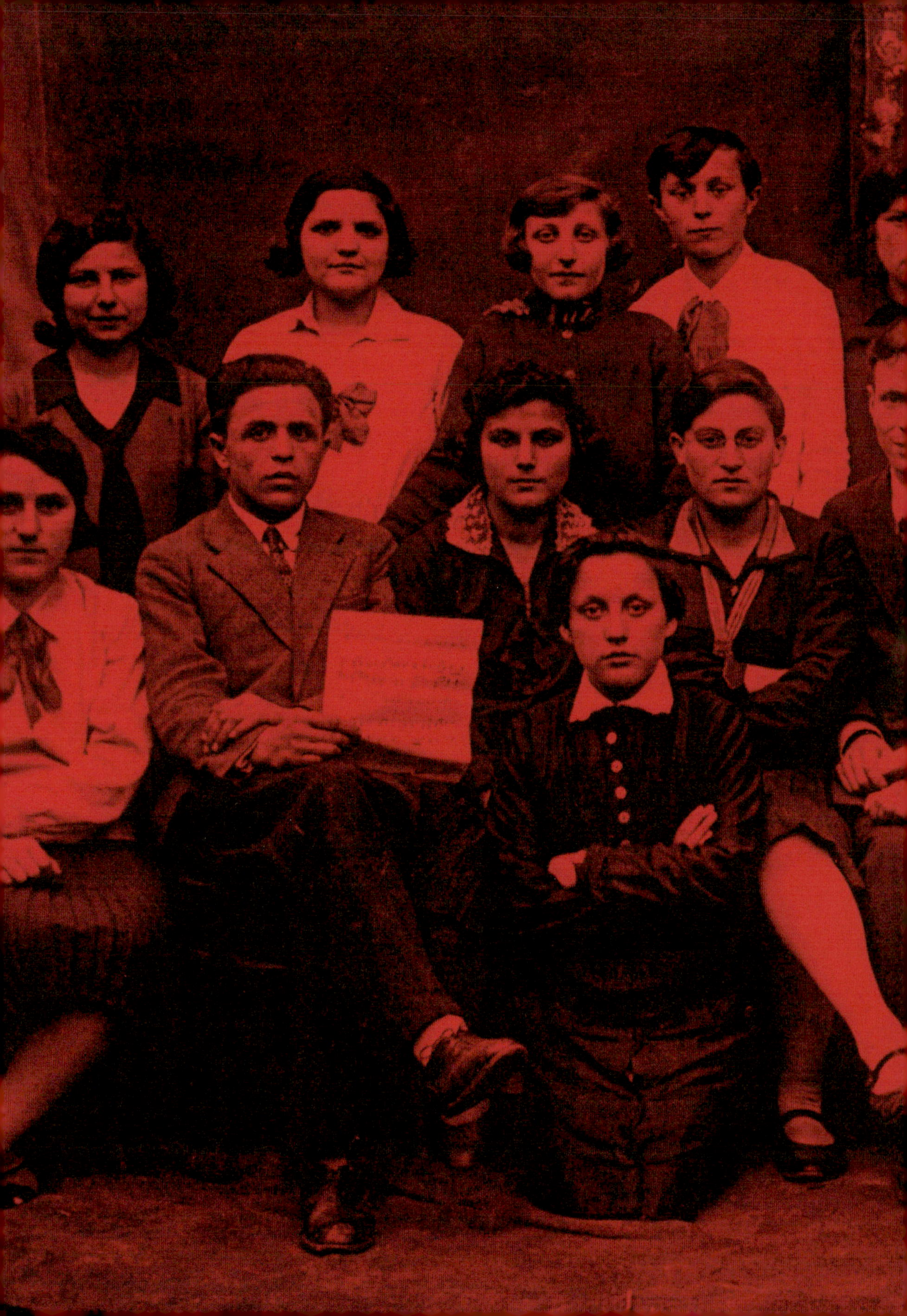

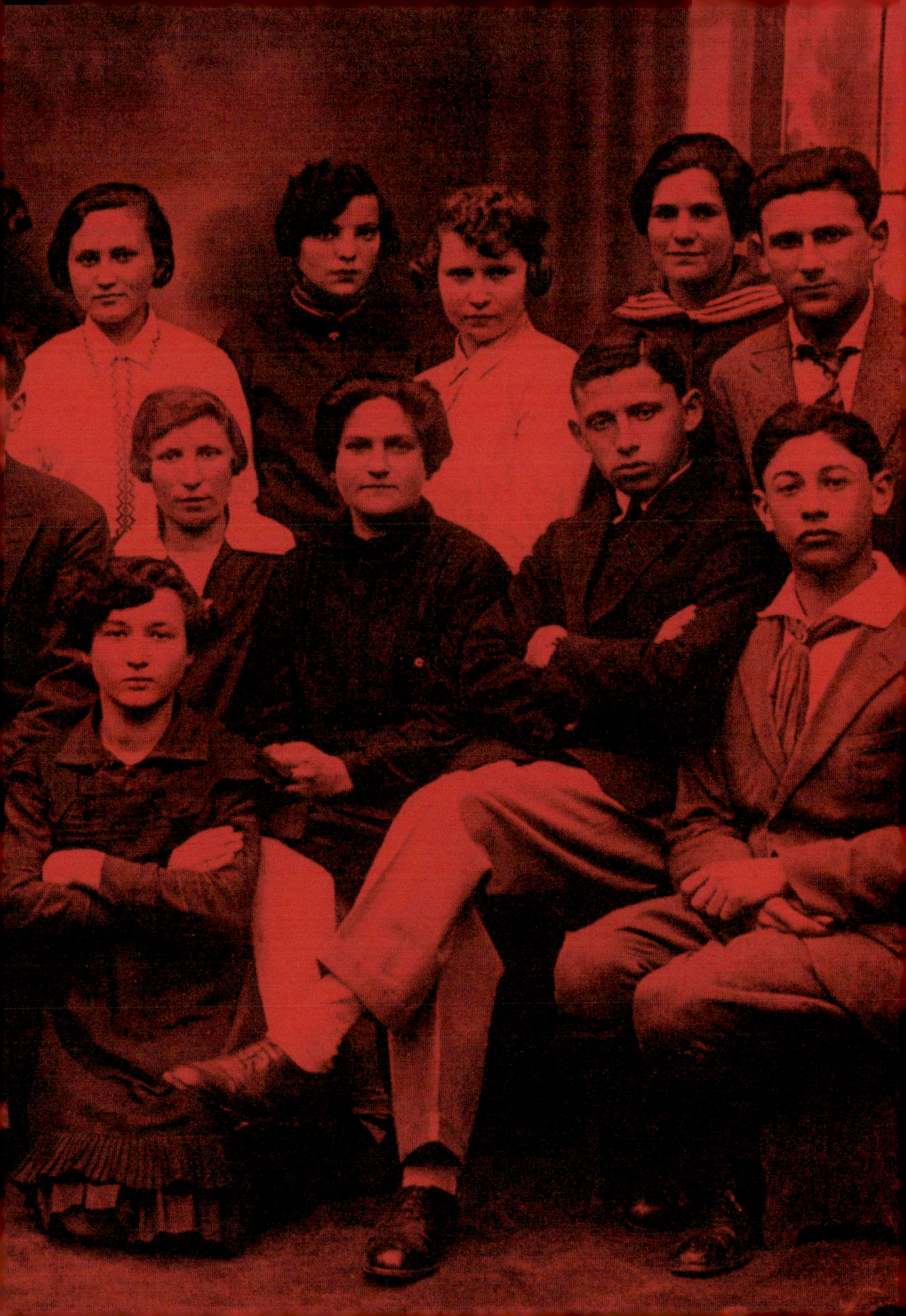

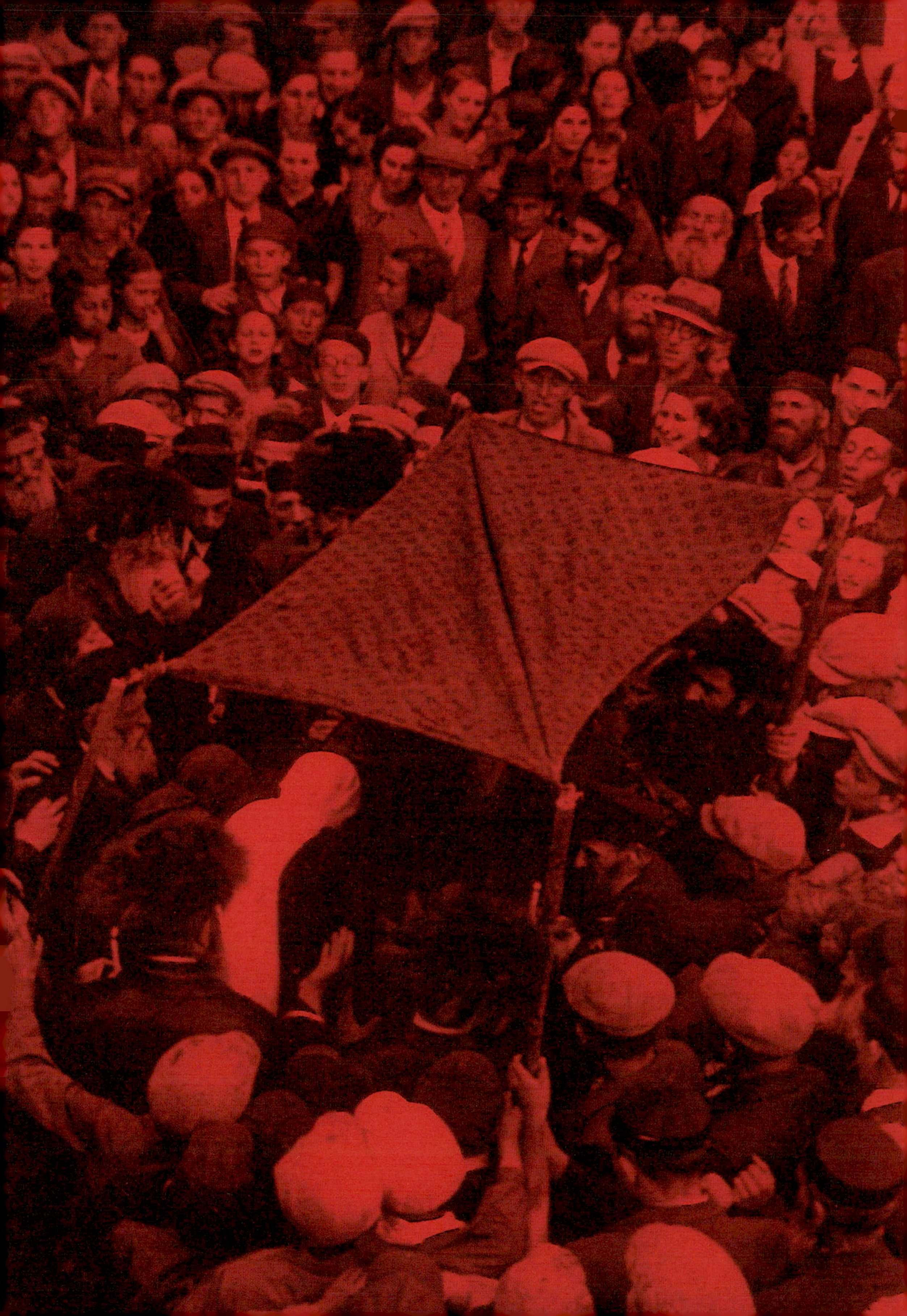

In the '70s, '80s, '90s, we were people, you know, and now we're Jews again.

It seems to be okay to be antisemitic at a certain level. But if more and more incidents take place in countries like France, in countries like Germany, in countries like the United States, then it will become easier for those who are inclined to do something similar to be accepted in a city like Toronto.

I don't know what the solution is, but I feel like a lot of it has to be led by policies. That's why you need a strong democracy, because individuals can have crazy ideas. If somebody is putting swastikas on synagogues, or Jewish community centers, they find them. This is a shameful thing that we don't believe in this culture. Because when you don't act on it, then you're saying, "It's just fine, go ahead. We wouldn't do it, but you know what, we understand where you're coming from." And then it's legitimized. So I think that it has to be through enforcement and policy and people standing up, every day.

Sometimes you just suss it out and are like, you know what, I feel like it might be inviting trouble to say I'm Jewish. It might not be, but why bring it up?

I just feel like I have to stand up to things. Although in my day-to-day life I don't experience it so much, but I feel you don't want to not be somewhere because you're scared to be there. But I've thought about it when I've gone to services. Like, is this the day that somebody loses their crap?

We have a teeny little backyard and it's right beside our neighbor's backyard. So on Shabbat occasionally, because the weather has been nice, we'll eat outside, and I'm accustomed throughout the Shabbat meal to keep my kippah on. But there have been a couple of times when I took it off because I felt uncomfortable about the neighbors seeing it. It's awful, but it's true.

I think there were maybe six Jews in the entire school. And I remember being harassed as a Jew on the streetcar going back and forth to school.

Before my interviews I was wearing a Star of David necklace and I decided to take it off because I didn't want any biases, or if anyone had any bad thoughts regarding individuals who are Jewish.

If anything, I make a point of saying I'm Jewish to put off, or to cut off, any mouthiness about Jews.

I was doing a job for *Toronto Life* on the community from Afghanistan. I saw this most beautiful scene of these two groups of picnickers, and the kids were running between the two carpets. The head guy said, "We're from Afghanistan. Why don't you take my picture?" He said to me, "Where are you from?" and I thought, this is a big Muslim gathering and I don't know how they're going to feel, or what they know, about people who are Jewish. I said, "Well I'm from Canada." And he goes, "No, no, no, where are you really from?"

We're not a monolith. Many of us have completely different perspectives but we sit down and have conversations as Jews all the time. Even in my own family we have different perspectives. So the idea that because you're Jewish you need to justify Israel's positions on things, or you need to explain Israel's positions . . . so that's the first situation in which I felt unsafe being Jewish; I felt misunderstood. Maybe that's not the right word. I felt like there wasn't enough safety around being Jewish.

I don't think I've been in a situation where I refrain from discussing Israel. If somebody doesn't like what I have to say, then that's fine. But people fought wars so that we could have freedoms to express how we feel. And they don't have to like everything I say, and I don't have to like everything they say, but I need to be able to have the opportunity to say it.

I tense up whenever it's mentioned in class because I just know that the knee-jerk reaction is for people to be hateful, and then I get defensive. I'm not in the mood to get into it with people who will end up just calling me a fascist or something, so I usually just avoid bringing it up.

I will hold back unless I understand there is a commitment to honesty, sincerity, and openness to dialogue. If I feel there's a risk that that isn't the case, I can make a decision to charge or hold back. In other words, take on the battle or not. And I have to assess on the spot.

My views are not always looked on by parts of the Jewish community with favour, and also parts of the non-Jewish community with favour. Occasionally I'll say something if I hear something that I find just so horrific to my core.

To tie it back to my mom's campaign, when people found out she was Jewish she got an abundance of questions on Israel. It's as if you are personally responsible for their actions just because you are Jewish.

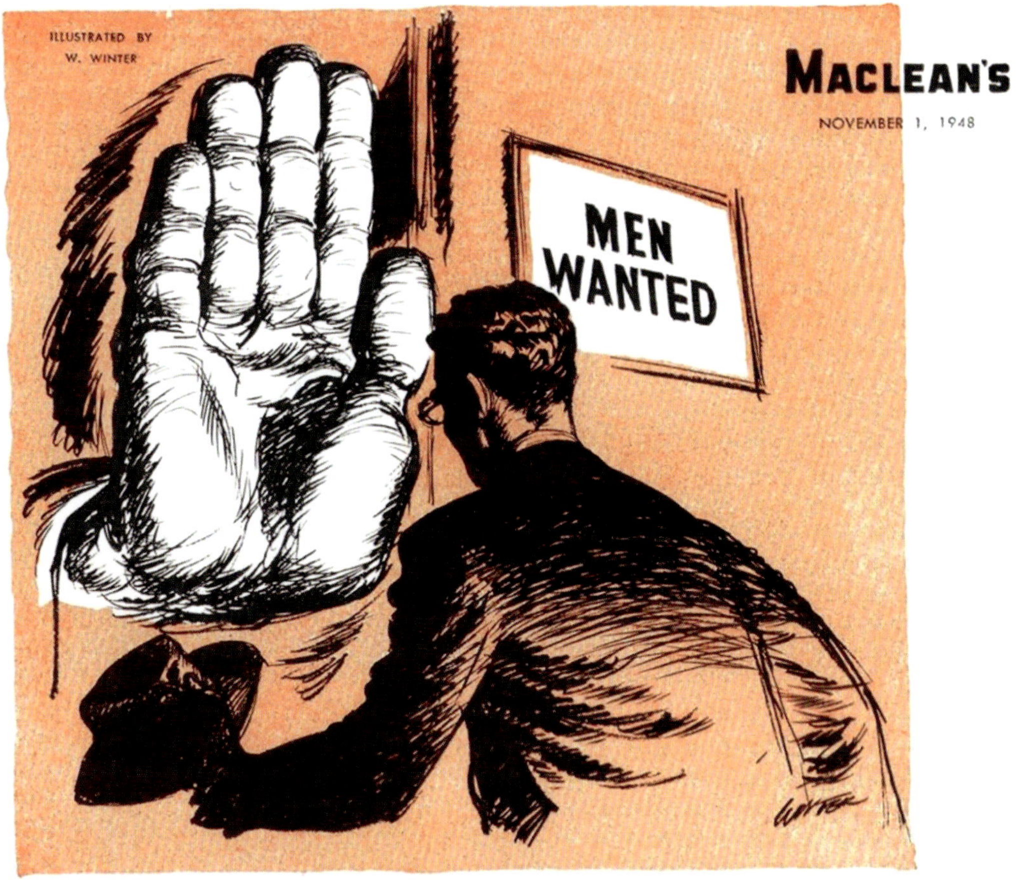

MACLEAN'S
NOVEMBER 1, 1948

No Jews Need Apply

By PIERRE BERTON

IN THE wartime winter of 1942, when employers of all kinds were desperate for men, a young accountant named Norman Lyons, who had been rejected for military service on medical grounds, started looking for a job.

Lyons was sent by the Unemployment Insurance Commission to a large war plant in Toronto which needed several accountants. After an interview by company officials, he was told there were no vacancies.

He phoned the personnel manager of a second war plant, giving his qualifications in detail. The personnel man said he was looking for a man like Lyons—there was a timekeeper's job available and several accountants' jobs open. When Lyons went around, the personnel man's face changed: Lyons wouldn't want the job, he said—the hours were long, the pay was low and he knew he wouldn't be interested. He didn't even bother to take Lyons' name and address.

Lyons tried a well-known accounting firm. The man he saw read his references, told him he'd have no trouble placing him immediately, said there was a crying need for men like him. Then, as an afterthought, he asked: "By the way, Mr. Lyons, what is your religion?" When Lyons told him, the company representative said sorry, there was nothing for him.

Lyons tried a second accounting firm. He was told: "There's no use beating about the bush. We don't employ Jews here."

The dilemma of Norman Lyons, who represents one of our most important minorities (there are more than 170,000 Jews in Canada, 1¼% of the population), has in the past half dozen years suddenly become a number one topic of conversation. A rash of books, plays, movies and radio broadcasts has dealt with the problem of anti-Semitism. Because of "Gentlemen's Agreement" and "Crossfire" and "Earth and High Heaven," people are doing more talking and thinking about this particularly vicious expression of race prejudice than ever before. Has the situation, then, changed since Norman Lyons went out looking for a job?

Race prejudice is a difficult thing to measure statistically, but Maclean's made a stab at it a month ago in an effort to find out what comparative job opportunities there were for Gentile and Jew in a particular field.

Two experienced girls with similar backgrounds and training were selected to answer newspaper advertisements for stenographers, typists, book keepers and filing clerks. These occupations we chosen because they cut right across the industr and business field from insurance companies truck manufacturers and because there is present a great shortage of experienced help in t secretarial field.

One of the girls took the name of Greenberg, the other of Grimes. The girl with the Jewish-sounding name phoned a prospective *Continued on page 53*

Ghettos in Canada? Or pogroms? Hardly. But try looking for a job — in engineering, say — if your name is Greenberg

SECOND SECTION

TORONTO DAILY STAR

TORONTO, TUESDAY, JUNE 22, 1937

JEWS NOT SURPRISED AS THEY ARE BANNED BY ST. ANDREW'S CLUB

Rabbi Sachs Declares It Is Another Manifestation of Old Racial Prejudice

PLAY AT WESTON

The banning of Jewish players from the pay-as-you-play course at St. Andrew's Golf club does not surprise prominent Jewish citizens who to-day said that Jews are not admitted to membership in any private Toronto golf club.

"There is a club at Weston called the Oakdale Golf club which is for Jewish players only," H. M. Swartz of the Jewish Daily Journal, told The Star. "As to the action of the St. Andrew's club, I can only say that after ten years in which Jewish people were welcome, their stand needs some explanation. I think, of course, that the club has the right to decide who shall play over its grounds. But when the club was young and struggling, remember, all players, whatever their race, were welcome."

Rabbi Samuel Sachs said the ban on Jewish players was just another manifestation of the old racial prejudice against Jews.

"I advise my people not to go where they are not wanted," he said. "They can play at the course in Weston. I do not think there is any real cause for the club's action, especially as Jewish men had a great deal to do with the building up of the course."

James J. Reid, secretary of the club, denied that there was a sign at the entrance of the links banning Jewish players.

"We put up a sign in the locker room, and one in the office," he declared. "The signs, which were printed read, 'After June 20th this club will be operated for Gentile patronage only.' We have no Jews among club members. All those who came here did so on the pay-as-you-play basis. We have several hundred Gentiles who play here regularly, and the club is about ten years old. The sign, which was put up Saturday, is only in line with the policy of other clubs in the city

(Continued on Page 21, Col. 1)

SAY CUTTEN MILLIONS NOT SENT TO CANADA

Judge Authorizes Sale of $300,000 Worth of Stock

Chicago, June 22.—Probate Judge John F. O'Connell approved to-day the sale of approximately $300,000 worth of stock in the estate of Arthur W. Cutten, grain speculator who died June 24, 1936. Cutten was a native of Guelph, Ont.

Dwight H. Green, attorney for the executor; Arthur Evans, trust officer, and I. J. Berkson, attorney for Harry A. Ash, a creditor, were expected back to-day from Guelph, where they sought allegedly hidden assets.

Ash, who had a $158,000 claim resulting from a trading deal, alleged Cutten told him before he died that he had transferred securities worth Millions of dollars to Canada. A hearing on these claims, denied by the Cutten family, was scheduled for July 16.

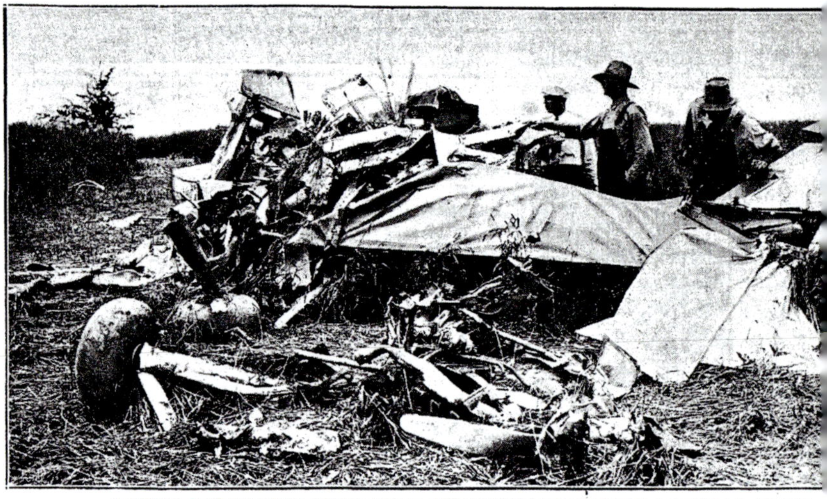

MANGLED WRECKAGE OF AEROPLANE IN WHICH THREE TORONTO MEN CRASHED TO DEATH

Federal aviation officials are trying to determine the cause of the air crash yesterday near St. Marys which claimed the lives of three Toronto men, Arthur Leavens, the pilot and his two companions, Charles Sockett and A. L. Ogden, both expert pilots. Observers of the accident said the aeroplane appeared to lose a wing while still in the air and then hurtled to earth completely out of control. The machine did not nose into the ground but apparently smashed along on its side, cutting a huge swath in the wheat. The swath can be seen in the upper left hand corner of the photograph. The bodies of the victims were badly mangled and officials had to move the aeroplane to extricate the the crash could mile away. Th ing from Toront

PITIFUL CRIES | ABBEY CHAIRS WORRY TO TORONTO DOCTOR | ALONG TURF. | CARS KILL MAIM | BIRTH CON

Anthony Koch @Anthony__Koch · Follow

Centennial Park in Toronto today.

Clearly this is just about freeing Palestine.

No Jew hatred whatsoever.

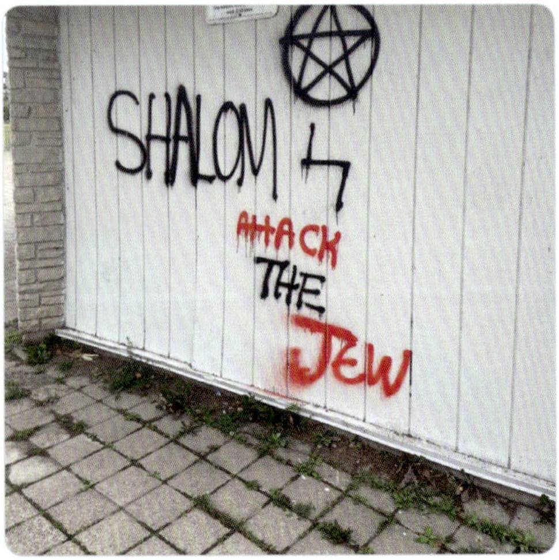

3:26 PM · Oct 15, 2023

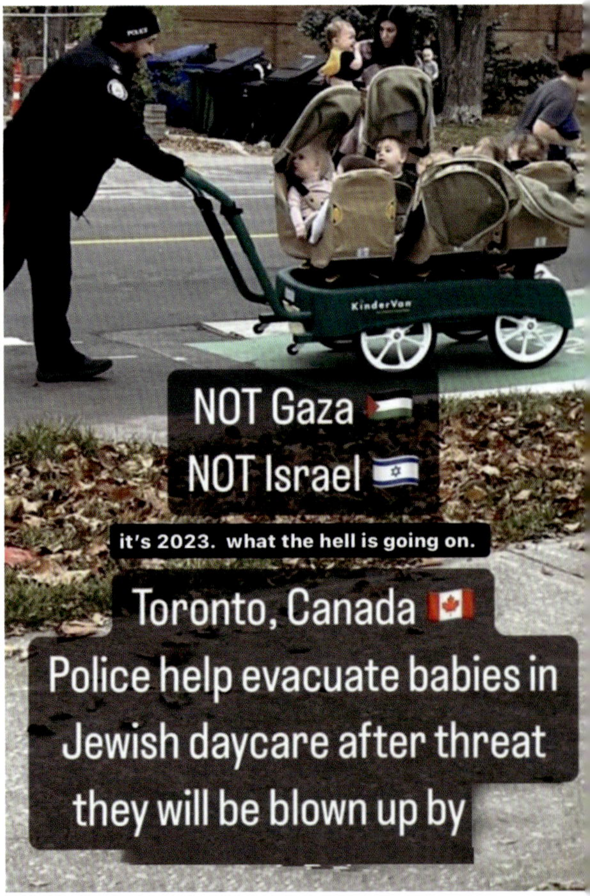

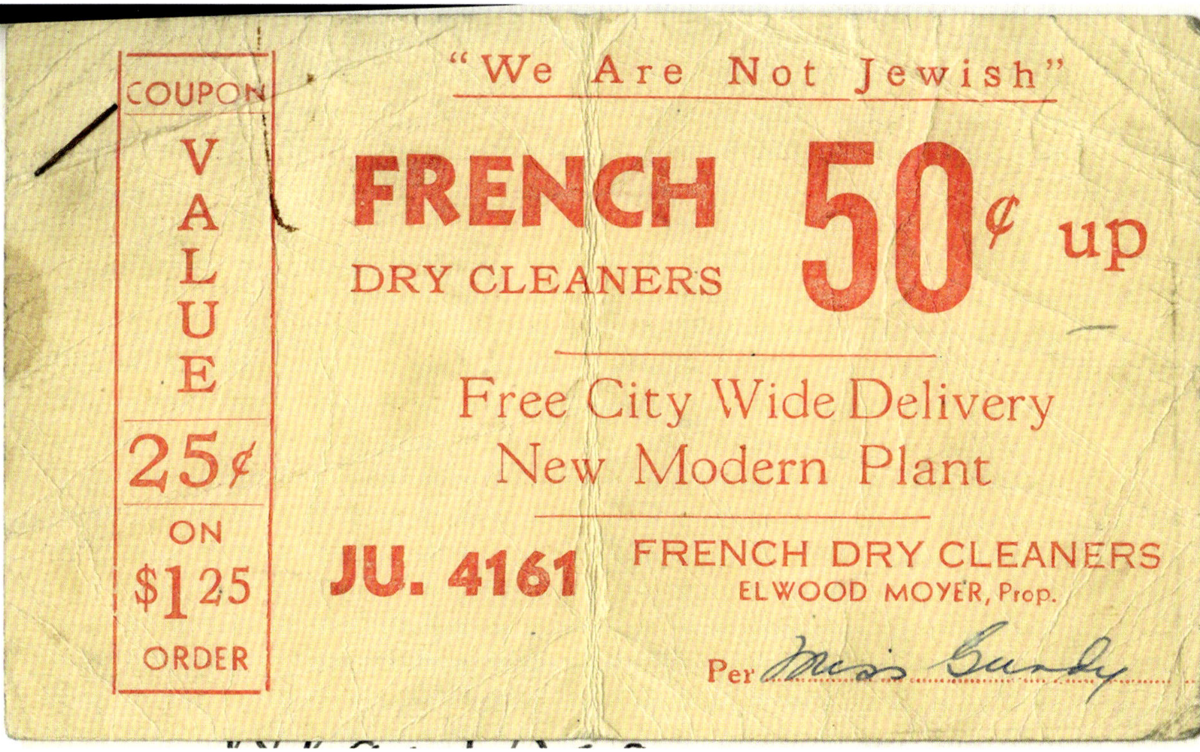
COUPON
VALUE
25¢
ON
$1.25
ORDER
"We Are Not Jewish"
FRENCH
DRY CLEANERS
50¢ up
Free City Wide Delivery
New Modern Plant
JU. 4161
FRENCH DRY CLEANERS
ELWOOD MOYER, Prop.
Per

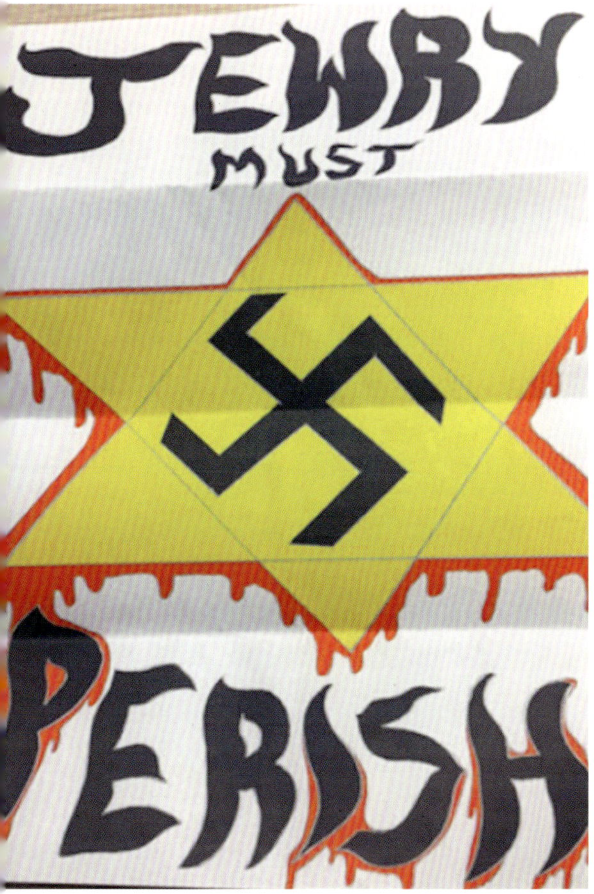
JEWRY
MUST
PERISH

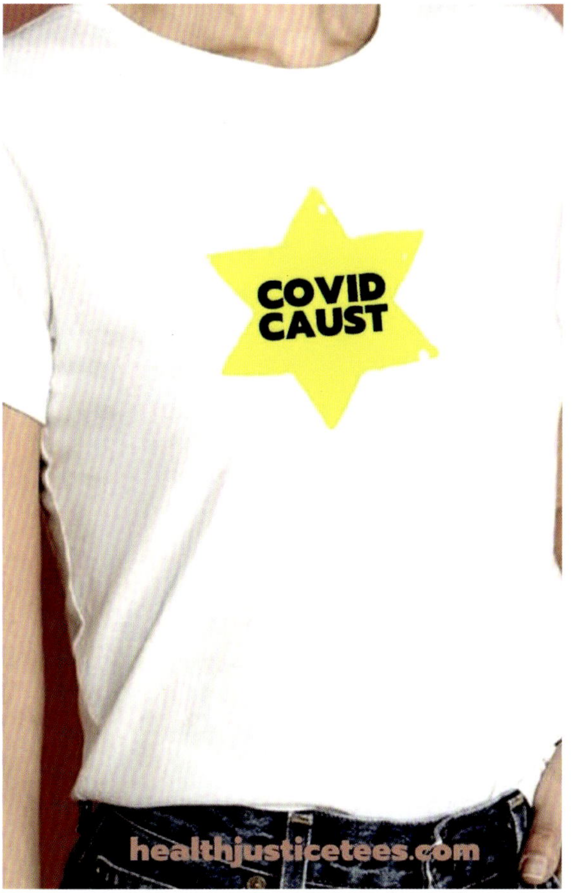
COVID
CAUST
healthjusticetees.com

Ki. 5758
Phone ~~Adelaide 4730~~

We specialize in Tinting and Hairdyeing, Marcelling
Scalp and Facial Treatments
Permanent Waving

Scarfe's French Beauty Shop

~~3 DUNDAS STREET EAST~~
~~Cor. Yonge St.~~ 64 Wellesley St.

Miss L. Noble.

When you applied at my place for a position you did not tell me you were Jewish. As I only can employ Gentiles I would not be able to employ you.

Yours
E. Scarfe

TORONTO
JUN 16
3 30 PM
1932
ONT.

Miss
Lillian Noble
258 Grace Street
Toronto

Fwd: FW: Scout Logistics Phone Interview - marnie.salsky@ryerson.ca - Ryerson University Mail

nbox&th=%23thread-f%3A1671669445767477145%7Cmsg-f%3A1671669445767477145&cvid=1

From: Wais M [mailto:wmassoumi@gmail.com]
Sent: April 2, 2014 11:07 AM
To: dani Etkin
Subject: Re: Scout Logistics Phone Interview

I don't work for Jews.

Best of luck in your search.

Wais

On Apr 2, 2014, at 10:45 AM, dani Etkin <dani@scoutlogistics.com<mailto:dani@scoutlogistics.com>> wrote:

Hi,

I am from Scout Logistics and have received you resume and would like to conduct a brief phone interview for the Sales Manager position this week, or next week if need be. I am in the office daily between 8am-5pm.

Please email me back confirming your telephone number and an ideal time to chat so I can contact you.

Thank you,

Dani Etkin-Spigelman

"The one thing that doesn't abide by majority rule is a person's conscience."
- Atticus Finch "To Kill a Mocking Bird"

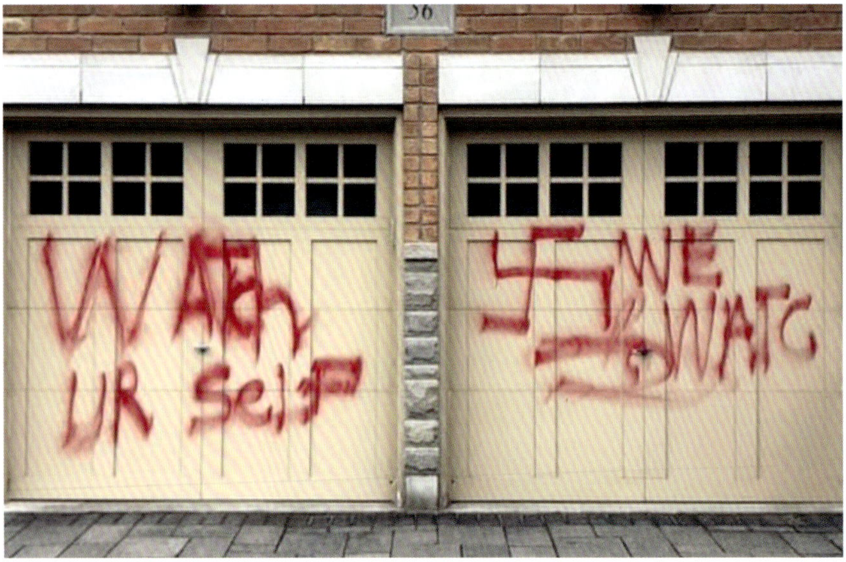
UR Self
WE
WATC

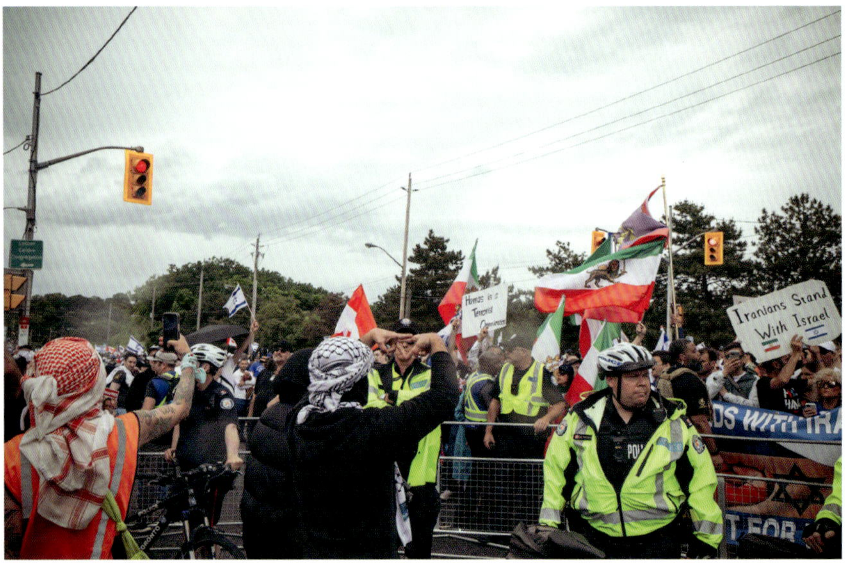
Iranians Stand
With Israel

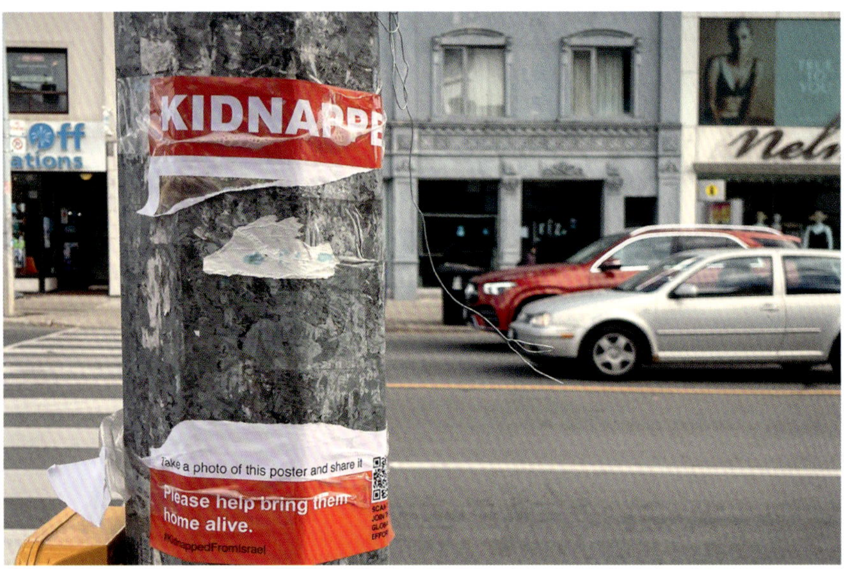
KIDNAPPE
Take a photo of this poster and share it
Please help bring them
home alive.
#KidnappedFromIsrael

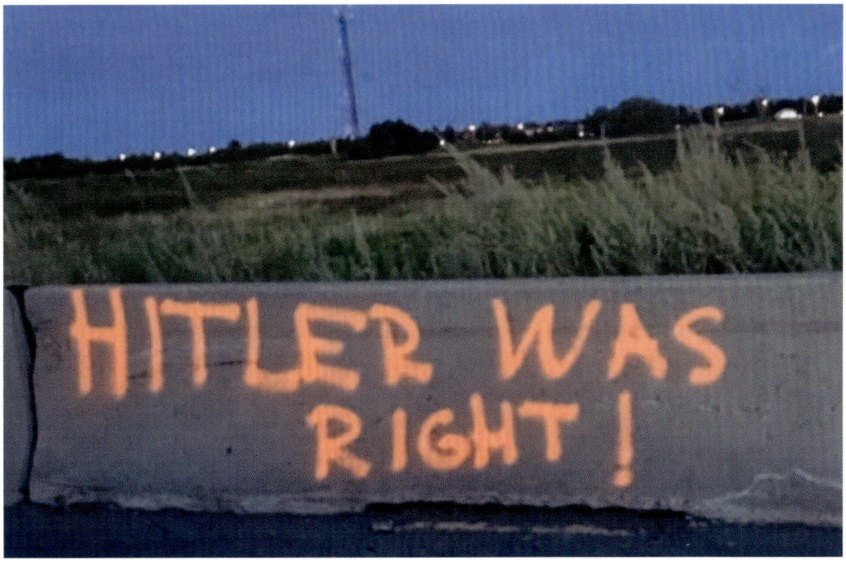
HITLER WAS
RIGHT!

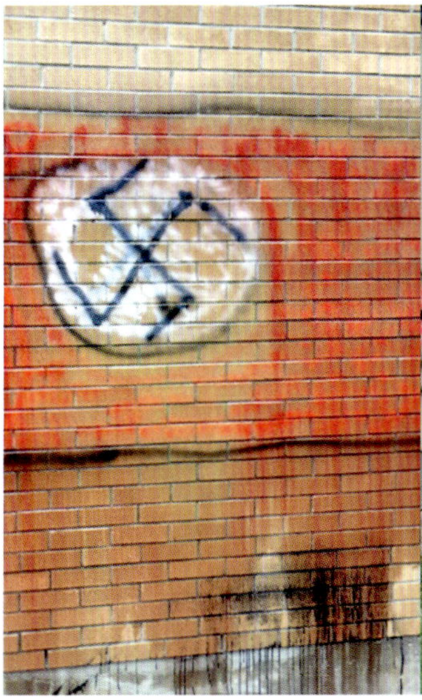

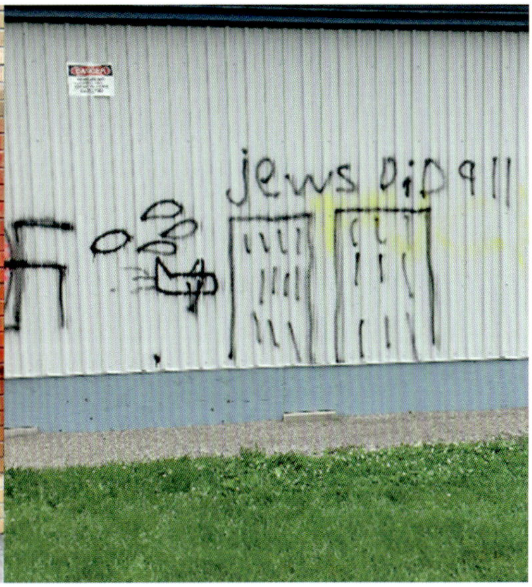
jews Did 911

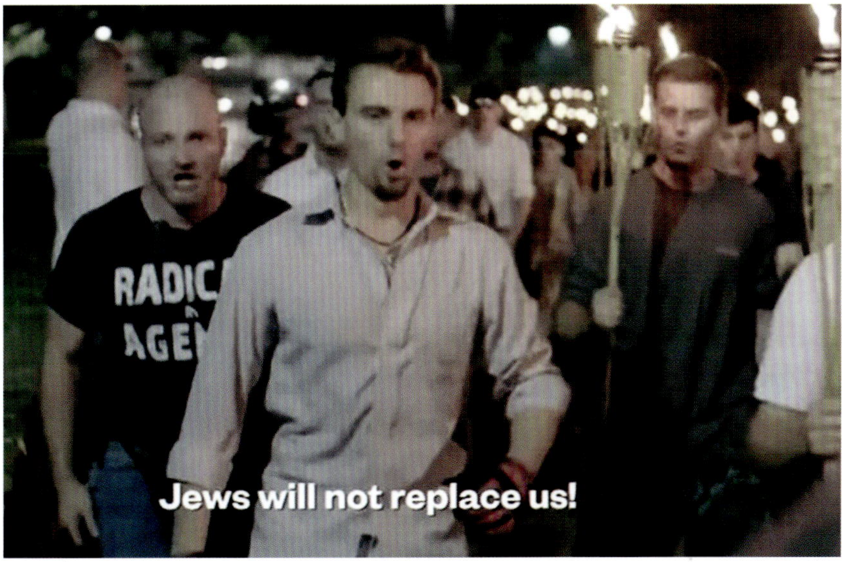
Jews will not replace us!

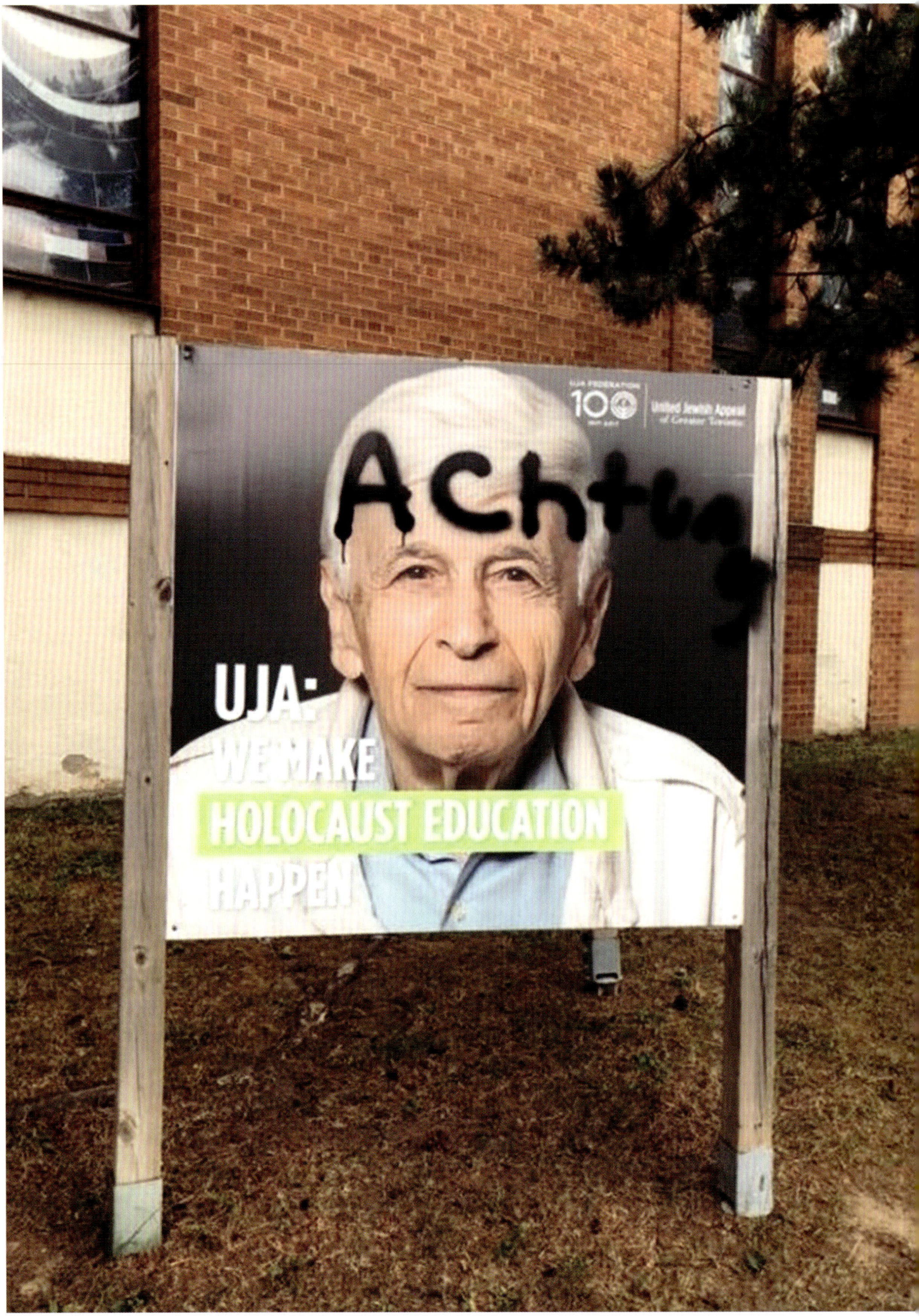
UJA FEDERATION
100
United Jewish Appeal of Greater Toronto
Achtung
UJA:
WE MAKE
HOLOCAUST EDUCATION
HAPPEN

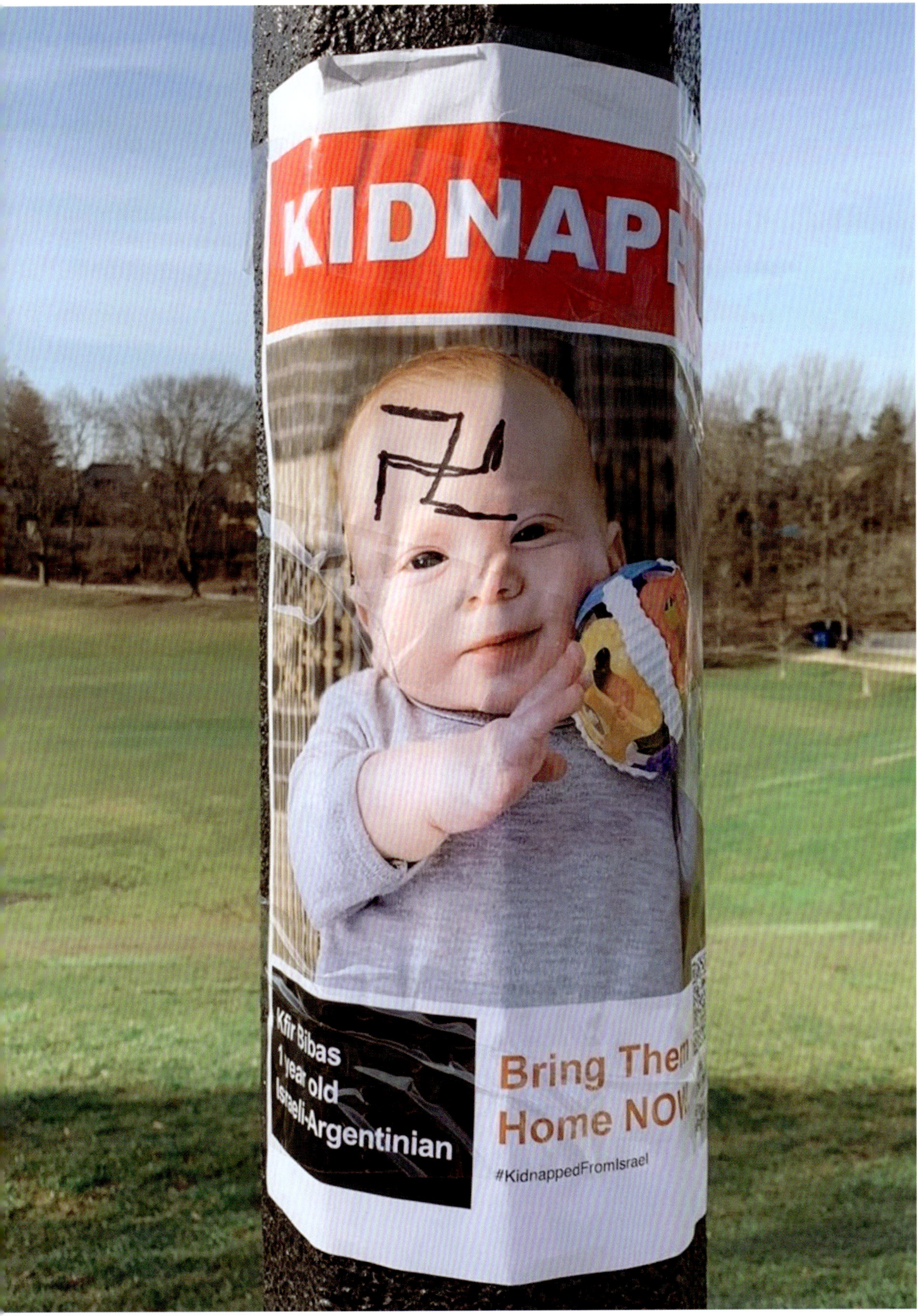
KIDNAPP
Kfir Bibas
1 year old
Israeli-Argentinian
Bring Them
Home NOW
#KidnappedFromIsrael

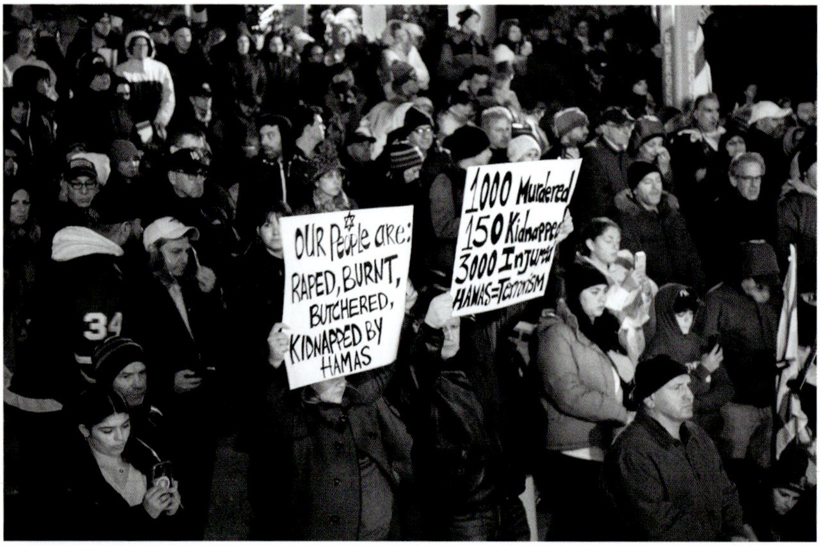
OUR People are:
RAPED, BURNT, BUTCHERED, KIDNAPPED BY HAMAS
1000 Murdered
150 Kidnappe
3000 Injured
HAMAS=Terrorism

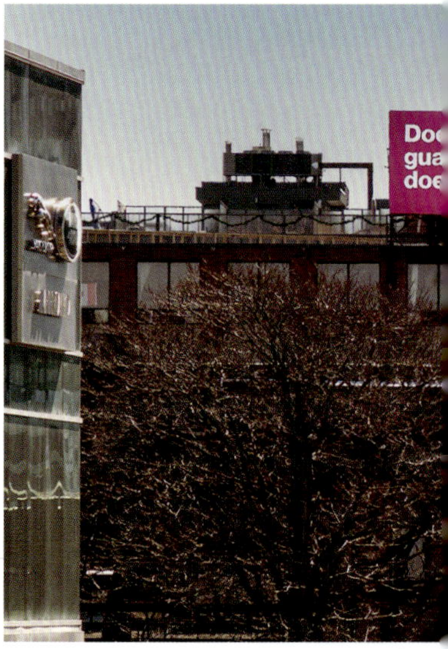

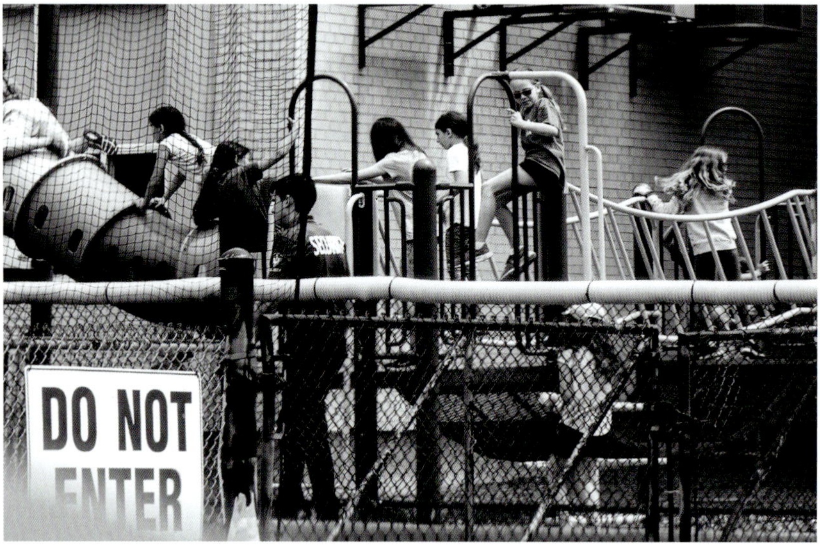
DO NOT
ENTER

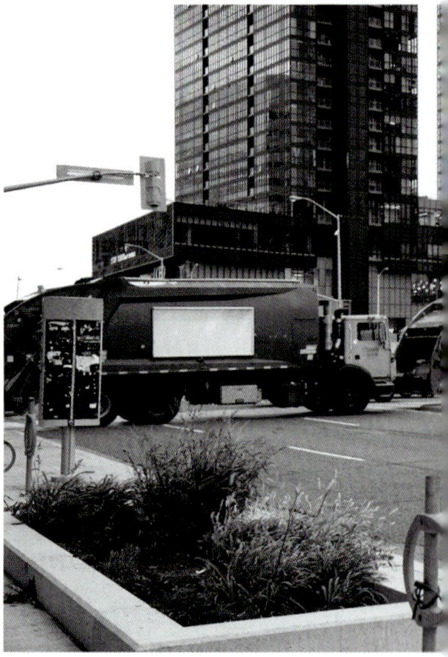

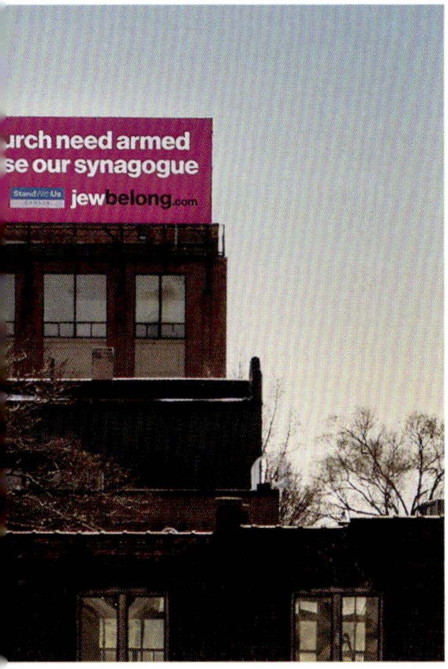
urch need armed
se our synagogue
jewbelong.com

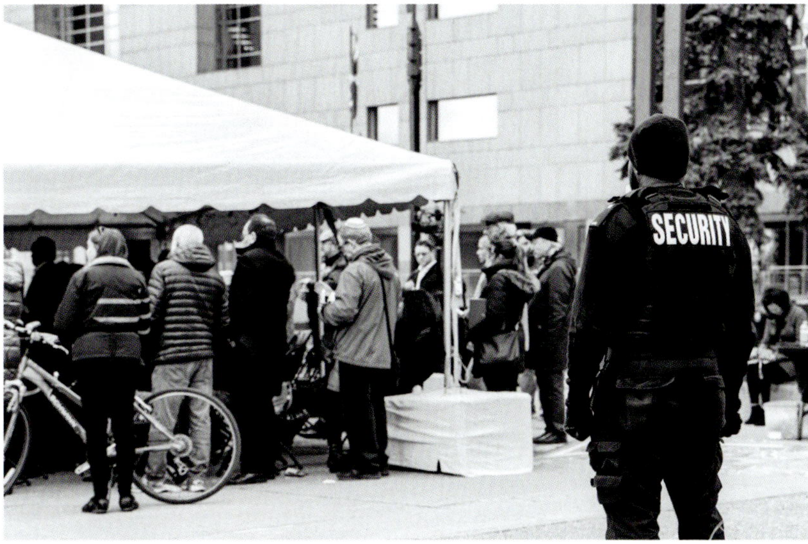
SECURITY

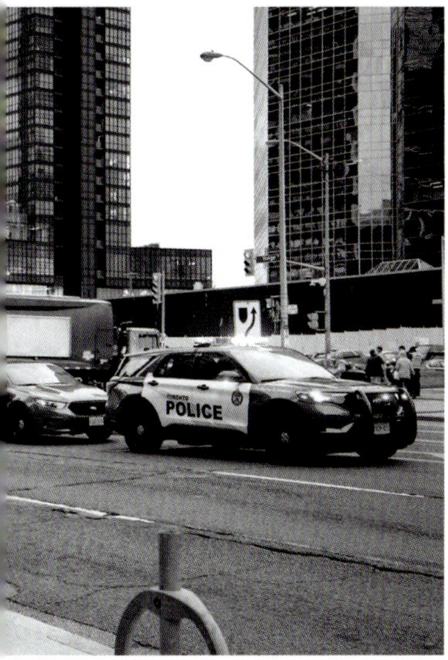
POLICE

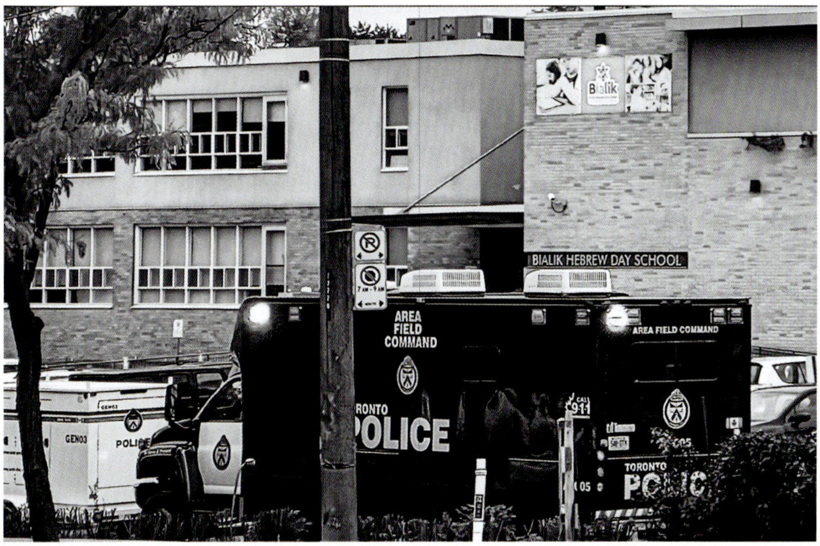
Bialik
BIALIK HEBREW DAY SCHOOL
AREA FIELD COMMAND
AREA FIELD COMMAND
POLICE

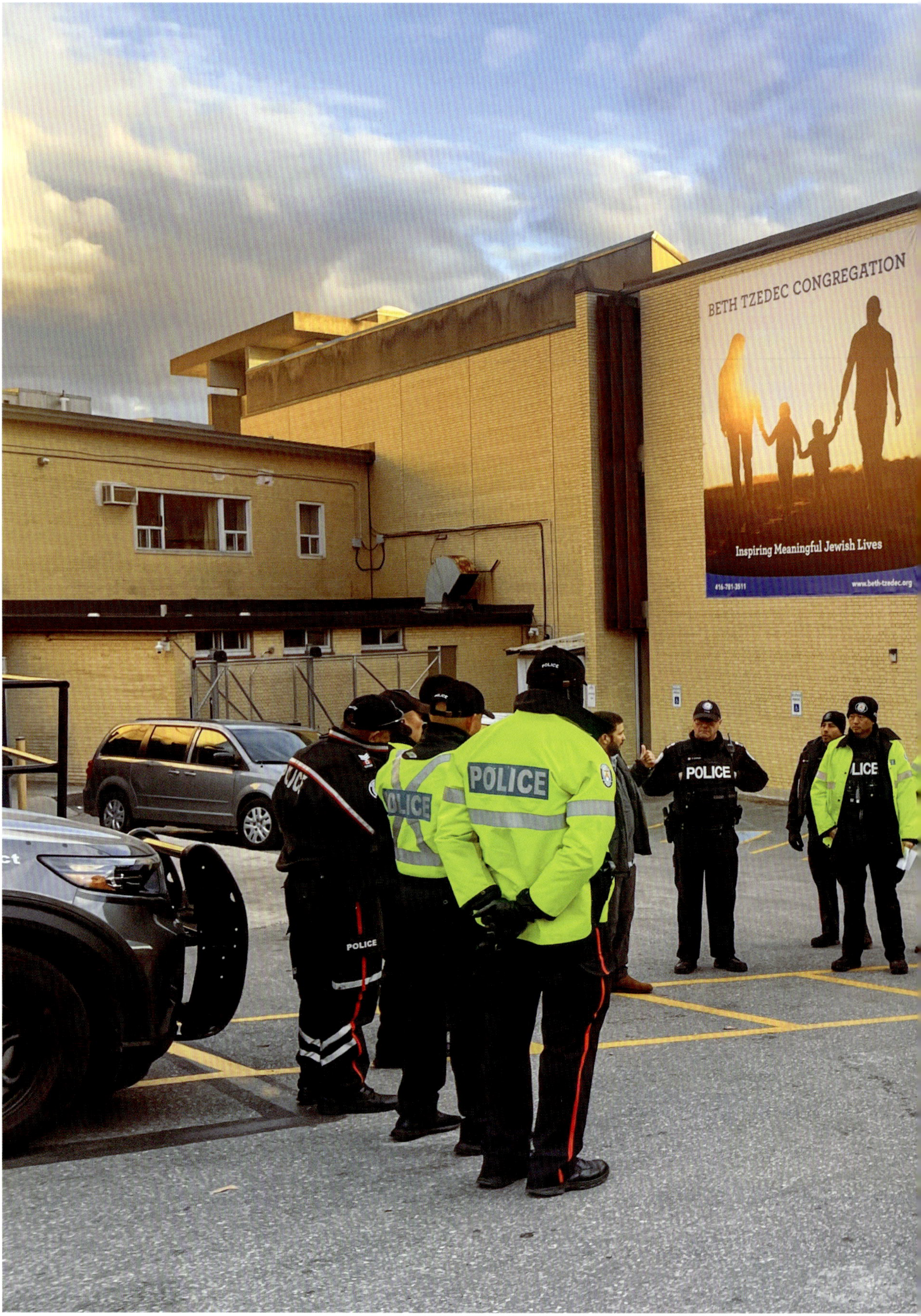
BETH TZEDEC CONGREGATION
Inspiring Meaningful Jewish Lives
www.beth-tzedec.org
POLICE
POLICE
POLICE

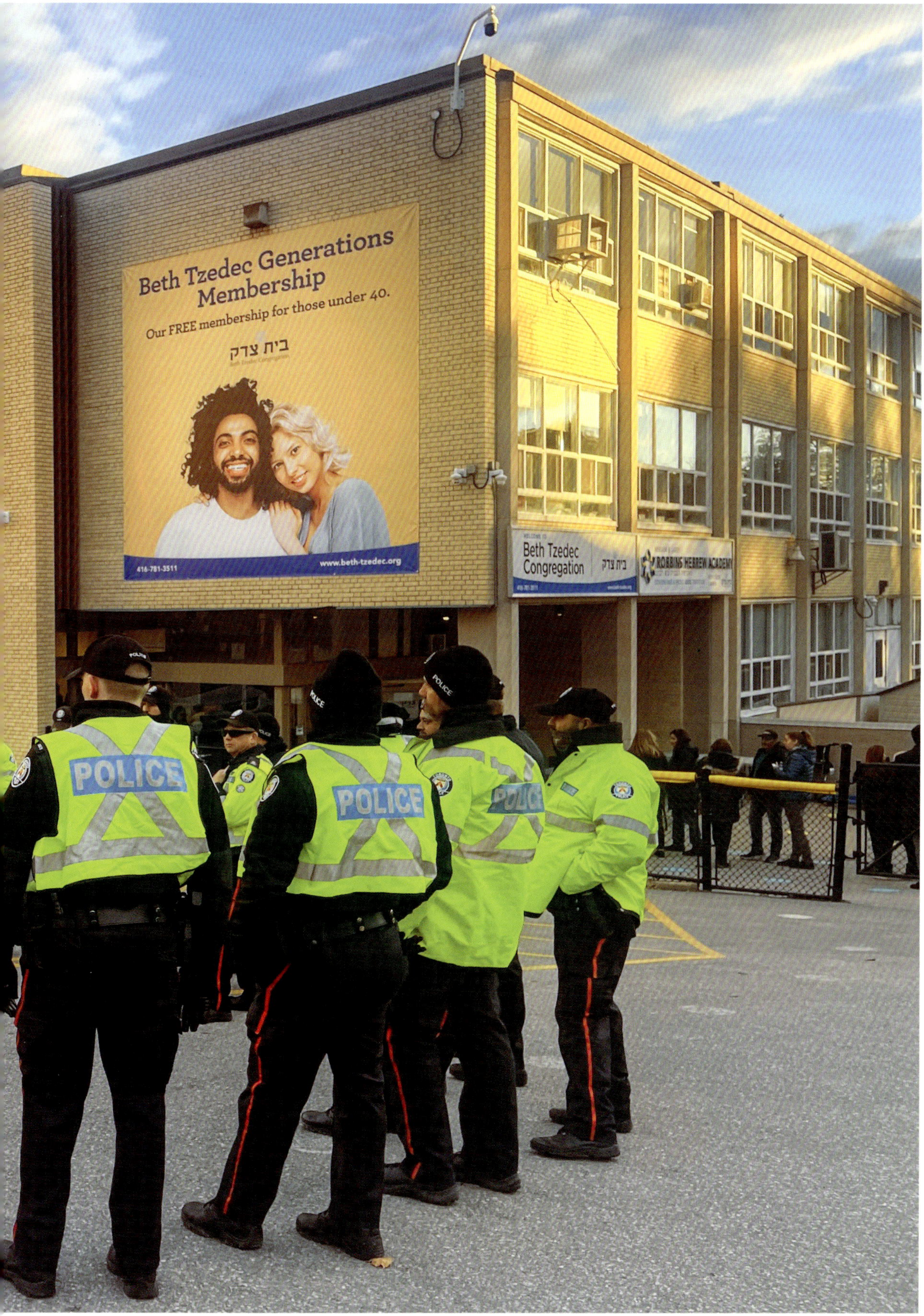
Beth Tzedec Generations Membership
Our FREE membership for those under 40.
בית צדק
416-781-3511
www.beth-tzedec.org
Beth Tzedec Congregation
בית צדק
ROBBINS HEBREW ACADEMY
POLICE
POLICE

CIJA ✔
@CIJAinfo

#JewishPrivilege has, for years, existed as an antisemitic theme used primarily by conspiracy theorists. Too many times, these conspiracy theories have ended with violence.

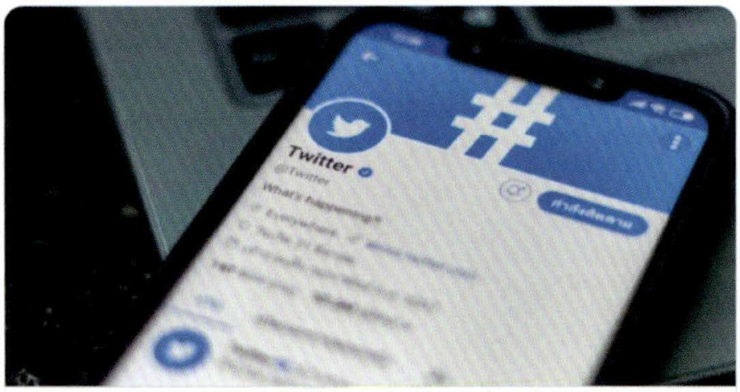

'JewishPrivilege' hashtag trends on Twitter as users fight back against anti-Se...
The anti-Semitic hashtag 'JewishPrivilege' was trending on Twitter Monday after Jewish people took it over to share their experiences of discrimination, ...
ctvnews.ca

Ariella Daniels (אריאלה דניאלס)
@AriellaDan18

#JewishPrivilege is when my grandmother and her family fled Karachi, Pakistan shortly after the partition, to escape attacks on the Jewish community. The synagogue was destroyed, their homes and property taken. All that is left is a cemetery and silence. ✡️

Lindsay 🇨🇦🌎📚✍️🛩️🌈✡️
@lindssoberano

#JewishPrivilege is standing in a room and others making Jew jokes in front of me because no one knows I'm Jewish ...

Storm B
@stormb0401

My #JewishPrivilege is that my great grandparents were born in the US and did not experience the Holocaust.

But that's because their parents fled Russia in the early 1900s to avoid persecution for being Jewish.

BrooklynBen
@BrooklynBen

#JewishPrivilege? Mine is easy. No matter what we all achieve, the most famous member of my Stanford class will always be Daniel Pearl, who was told to say to the camera "My name is Daniel Pearl and I am a Jew" as his last words, before he was beheaded on camera by Al Qaeda.

randi bergman ✔
@randibergman

being asked if i was jewish at a wedding and after i said yes, him lifting a glass to me and cheersing with "death to israel" #JewishPrivilege

Shoshanna Keats Jaskoll
@skjask

#JewishPrivilege is my daughter using her great grandfather's Aushweitz tattoo number as her computer passcode

> **Ashager Araro** @AshagerAraro · 19h
> #JewishPrivilege it not knowing my grandfather from my mother's side, because he was murdered for being Jewish in Ethiopia.
> twitter.com/HenMazzig/stat...

Rev. Michael Coren
@michaelcoren

For those who claim that anti-Semitism is all due to Israeli actions how does this explain:
1)Medieval massacres and expulsions
2)Inquisition
3)Pogroms
4)Holocaust
All, I think, before 1948.
Be well and be blessed.
#Jews

B
@Byrun_nuryB

I'm not Jewish, but b/c of my last name there are anti-semites who have assumed my Dad & I were/are. We've both experienced anti-semitism 1st hand, & we are both proud to have been confused for Jewish. Fuck anti-semites, their blind hatred, & galling ignorance.
#JewishPrivilege

Love, Ari
@Ari_bacher

I will never stop being proud of being Jewish. The community, culture, traditions and values that being a Jew has taught/given me overpowers all the hate poured out on the #JewishPrivilege hashtag.

Ryan
@ryanazr

#JewishPrivilege is when a non-Jew like myself tried wearing a Kippah for a couple of months to understand how my Jewish friends feel only to face numerous anti-Semitic incidents, one of the instance being getting shouted by a white man: "stupid Jew, go get gassed."

Combat Anti-Semitism
@CombatASemitism

#antisemitism is a global problem. Canadian #Jewishprivilege: Despite making up 1% of the population, 19% of all police-reported hate crimes in 2018 were targeted at Jews. This horrifying statistic makes Jews the most targeted religious minority in Canada.

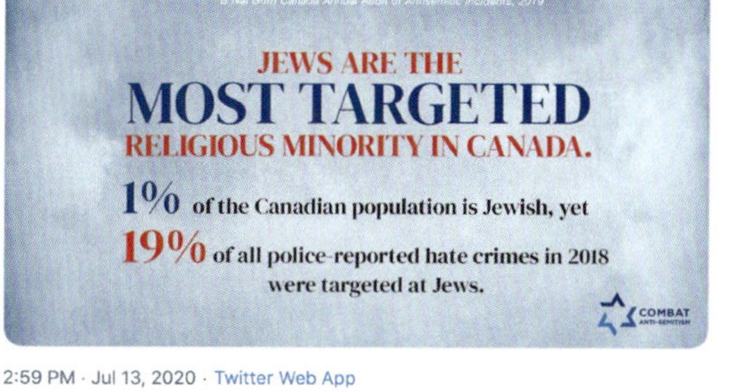

2:59 PM · Jul 13, 2020 · Twitter Web App

Security ramping up at Canadian schools, synagogues and community centres

Toronto police hate crimes unit investigates after three arrested at Jewish high school

FRÉDÉRIK-XAVIER DUHAMEL
ALANNA SMITH
LAURA STONE

The Toronto police department's hate crimes unit is investigating after the arrest of three people at a Jewish high school, as police forces, synagogues, mosques and schools across the country announced heightened security measures in the wake of last week's attack against Israel.

Police forces in several cities announced increased patrols of places of worship and cultural centres after a former Hamas leader called for a "general mobilization" of Muslims to protest against the retaliatory bombing by Israel of Gaza. The Toronto District School Board was one of several in the country to reassure parents that safety was being prioritized as religious leaders described a climate of fear and anxiety from a conflict that has killed thousands, including at least three Canadians.

On Thursday, three male suspects allegedly made undisclosed verbal threats at the Community Hebrew Academy of Toronto and were arrested by Toronto police, the force said in a statement. The hate crimes unit is now investigating. Other police agencies across Canada, including those in Montreal, Vancouver, Edmonton, Halifax, Saskatoon and Winnipeg, said they were unaware of any hate-motivated crimes but most have been on high alert after the weekend's attacks in Israel, the continuing war against Hamas, and related tensions and protests in Jewish and Palestinian communities across Canada.

Toronto Police Chief Myron Demkiw said in a press conference Thursday that additional patrols in and around Jewish communities and places of worship will continue for the foreseeable future. He said leaders from the Jewish and Palestinian communities have expressed that the overseas war "has shaken their feelings of peace and security, here at home."

Chief Demkiw added that the hate crimes unit will "aggressively pursue" any alleged or suspected hate-fuelled incidents.

On the East Coast, Halifax Regional Police spokesperson John MacLeod said in a statement that "the escalation of violence in the Middle East is a great concern" to the community. He said there has been no specific threat to public safety in the region but police are on alert. In Manitoba, the Winnipeg Police Department said it has also increased patrols at places deemed to be higher-risk, such as places of worship, and the service continues to have a visible presence at rallies and protests.

In Victoria, officers were assigned to monitor a prayer vigil for Israel on Thursday night. And in Vancouver, Sergeant Steve Addison said there was no specific threat to any location in the city but said police know many residents are concerned for their safety.

Montreal's police service said in a statement it, too, was making officers visible "around places of worship and other places of interest," but said there is "no significant increase" in complaints related to the events of the past week, despite one incident posted online Wednesday that quickly went viral.

> Toronto Police Chief Myron Demkiw said in a press conference Thursday that additional patrols in and around Jewish communities and places of worship will continue for the foreseeable future.

In the video, a woman is seen verbally attacking another woman who had displayed a Palestinian flag on her vehicle. The second woman says her car was rammed. Montreal police spokesperson Jeanne Drouin confirmed the force is investigating the alleged hate crime and hit and run.

Calgary Imam Syed Soharwardy said he is fearful that the hate, division and fear-mongering by some political leaders and on social media will lead to real-life violence against Muslims in Canada.

He pointed directly at the June, 2021, truck attack in London, Ont., where four members of a Muslim family were killed in an alleged act of terrorism, that the accused told police was motivated by white-nationalist beliefs and was politically motivated.

Mr. Soharwardy said there is constant anxiety that an attack like this will happen again and that distressing images and videos of dead Israelis and Palestinians will deepen division. He is scared for both the Muslim and Jewish communities.

"In fear, somebody may react right and that reaction could be pretty destructive and could be very damaging for our country," he said. "Please stand up with peace. That's what is most important."

Yair Szlak, the president and chief executive officer of Federation CJA, a Jewish cultural and advocacy non-profit based in Montreal, said even without any specific threats, people are scared.

"In ordinary times, we always live in anxiety," he said. "In times like this ... we live in trepidation and fear."

Justice and public-safety ministers, meeting in Bromont, Que., on Thursday, issued a statement urging Canadians to remain united.

"Our law enforcement and security partners remain vigilant in the face of these potential disruptions and are monitoring the situation closely to ensure the safety of all Canadian citizens," it read.

Federal Minister of Public Safety Dominic LeBlanc said in a statement that Canada stands in solidarity with Jewish communities "ahead of the Hamas-led call for mobilization around the world." There is no place "for the glorification of violence or terror, here in Canada or around the world," he said, noting that Hamas is listed as a terrorist organization in Canada.

Conservative deputy leader Melissa Lantsman said her party wants the Liberal government to do more to ensure Jewish people are protected ahead of the perceived threat of protests.

"We've heard a lot of concern in the community, from Jewish-owned businesses operating whether their employees are comfortable coming to work. Parents who are unsure about sending their kids to either daycare or school," she said. "People are rightfully exercising a lot of caution."

Ms. Lantsman said she wants the government to convene an "urgent" call with provincial and municipal law enforcement to provide effective co-ordination, ensure the RCMP provides resources and intelligence to police agencies, and update Canadians on whether the federal threat assessment is being re-evaluated.

Youth arrested on terror-related charges appears in court

JEWISH TARGETS

Christopher Nardi

OTTAWA • An Ottawa youth who was arrested on the weekend on two terrorism-related charges targeting Jewish people is now facing three more charges, including two related to possession of explosives.

The young man, who cannot legally be identified because he is a minor, briefly appeared virtually at the Ottawa courthouse Monday, four days after he was arrested by the RCMP.

Saturday, the police force said he was charged with two counts of terrorism-related charges. The first was "facilitating a terrorist activity by communicating instructional material related to an explosive substance." The second was for allegedly indirectly or directly and knowingly instructing a person "to carry out a terrorist activity against Jewish persons."

By Monday, the youth faced a total of five charges, including a second charge related to facilitating a terrorist activity and two new charges relating to explosives.

The first is related to possession of explosives, and the second is for possessing them with intent to either "endanger life or to cause serious damage to property" or enable another person to do so.

It is not known if anyone else is being investigated in connection to the case.

The Jewish Federation of Ottawa said in an email to community members Sunday that police confirmed there is no risk to the community because the teen is now in custody.

Ottawa Police have increased patrols of Jewish institutions, including synagogues, community centres and schools. But the Jewish Federation said police continue to encourage the community to be vigilant.

"We ask that everyone exercise heightened awareness and (be) diligent in following security protocols," the email said.

The youth's lawyer in court Monday was Jon Doody, who recently represented convicted ex-RCMP leaker Cameron Ortis and has considerable experience in criminal and national security law.

The RCMP announced on Saturday that it had arrested the youth for terrorism-related offences that targeted "Jewish persons."

It also warned of a "concerning trend" of online violent extremism and terrorism in Canada.

"Since June 2023, the RCMP has arrested five young persons on terrorism-related offences — either terrorism related charges or laying of information for a Terrorism Offence Peace Bond," the RCMP said in a news release.

The youth's father told Global News Saturday that he had warned his son to stay clear of extremists and had sent him to consult with an imam.

The broadcaster also reported that a Facebook page that appeared to belong to the young man's father posted several derogatory posts about Jews and Zionists in Arabic, including one that called to get rid of all Israelis.

Saturday, Ottawa Mayor Mark Sutcliffe said on X (formerly Twitter) that police had averted a planned terror attack against the city's Jewish community.

"I was shocked to learn the details," Sutcliffe wrote on social media.

"I'm grateful and relieved that in this case, through strong investigative work, the RCMP and Ottawa Police were able to avert this planned event before it happened."

RCMP said the Canadian Security Intelligence Service and the Integrated Terrorism Assessment Centre, along with provincial and municipal police, provided "indispensable collaboration" in the case.

Amid the rise of violent extremism and terrorist use of the internet, the RCMP statement asked "adults in positions of authority" including parents, guardians, teachers and coaches, "to be alert for behaviours of concern which may be linked to violent extremism."

Jewish and Muslim leaders across Canada have reported an increase in hate-motivated attacks since the terrorist attacks launched by Hamas on Israel on Oct. 7, and the massive military response by Israel in Gaza.

National Post, with additional reporting by Canadian Press

Hate crime charges laid after doctor harassed

OTTAWA

MARLO GLASS

OTTAWA • A B.C. man has been charged with hate crimes after an Ottawa doctor said she received an antisemitic, misogynistic and intimidating phone call.

The Ottawa Police Service said on Monday a 39-year-old man faces charges of harassment, intimidation and indecent telecommunications after an investigation by the police force's Hate and Bias Crime Unit.

The man, whose name has not been released, is to appear in court in January.

None of the charges have been proven in court.

Police did not identify the victim, but in a social media post Monday Dr. Nili Kaplan-Myrth said her family medicine clinic received the threatening message on Aug. 28. She said she has made dozens of complaints to Ottawa police for "pretty vile" antisemitic comments, some of them threatening violence against her and her family.

Kaplan-Myrth, who is Jewish, said she has been the subject of antisemitism and threats on social media since she was elected as an Ottawa-Carleton District School Board trustee last year. She has been an outspoken advocate for LGBTQ+ rights and public health policies, including mask mandates.

A transcript of the phone message references the Holocaust and includes misogynistic slurs, as well as a threat to have Kaplan-Myrth's "(medical) licence pulled."

The three charges, she says, are "a tiny, tiny drop in the bucket" of threats she has received over the past year, with "pretty vile threats" against her and her family.

"Threat after threat to be killed or harmed, people threatening to destroy my career because I'm a Jew, a doctor, and helped thousands of people in Ottawa, to keep them healthy throughout the pandemic," she said in an interview. "And I stood up for transgender rights."

Kaplan-Myrth says she has increased security measures around her home and office following the harassment, but worries about the chilling effect harassment can have on public figures.

Kaplan-Myrth is also in a dispute with the school board. She filed a complaint with the Human Rights Tribunal of Ontario last week, alleging she had been subjected to antisemitic treatment that fellow trustees and senior board leaders didn't take seriously.

The school board's integrity commissioner has also recommended code of conduct sanctions against Kaplan-Myrth.

"I'm 49 years old, and until I stepped onto a public stage in order to help the community, I had never been subjected to any of these words," she said. "Why would any good person, whose heart is in the right place — to help the community — why would they step into politics?"

Postmedia News

OPINION

TORONTO STAR, ESTABLISHED 1892 — JOSEPH E. ATKINSON, PUBLISHER 1899 - 1948

THE STAR'S VIEW

Combating Holocaust denial

For evidence that Holocaust education is lacking in this nation, one need not look in a specific place because the evidence is everywhere.

It is in the vile antisemitic hate spewed on social media amid the Israel-Hamas war; it was in Canada's House of Commons in September, when lawmakers stood and applauded a former Nazi; and perhaps most concerning, it is among our youth who are increasingly misinformed about the genocide of six million Jews at the hands of the Nazis during the Second World War.

According to a recent survey of several thousand North American teens by Canadian Holocaust education advocacy group Liberation75, "32.9 per cent of students don't know what to think about the Holocaust, think the number of Jews who died has been exaggerated, or question whether the Holocaust even happened."

Many of the students polled reported getting their information about the Holocaust from social media — a poor source of credible information on the best of days.

According to the UN, which published a report on the many myriad ways social media fuels Holocaust denial, nearly 10 per cent of Holocaust-themed Facebook posts and 15 per cent of Holocaust-themed posts on X, the website previously called Twitter, engaged in denial and distortion.

There was, however, one hopeful piece in Liberation75's otherwise grim report:

"92.64 per cent of Ontario students said they wanted to learn more about the Holocaust."

It appears they will get their wish.

This month, Ontario's provincial government announced that starting in September 2025, lessons on the Holocaust will be expanded in Grade 10 history. Not only will these lessons cover the historical events surrounding the mass slaughter of Jews and other minority groups during the Second World War, but Education Minister Stephen Lecce said the lessons "will explicitly link the Holocaust to extreme political ideologies, including fascism, antisemitism in Canada in the 1930s and 1940s, and the contemporary impacts of rising antisemitism."

"By including new mandatory learning in Holocaust education in elementary and secondary schools, we are ensuring students are never bystanders in the face of hate and division," Lecce said in a statement.

This announcement from the provincial government comes on the heels of a similar announcement last year about the ministry's "first mandatory learning requirement in elementary school on Holocaust education in the Grade 6 curriculum."

These expansions are warranted and necessary for several reasons, among them the fact that while antisemitism is on the ascendent in Canada and abroad, the number of living Holocaust survivors is declining — and with them their stories.

According to the UN, which published a report on the many myriad ways social media fuels Holocaust denial, nearly 10 per cent of Holocaust-themed Facebook posts and 15 per cent of Holocaust-themed posts on X, engaged in denial and distortion

And it is critical for another reason: young people today consume most of their news online, often in the form of unverified videos and infographics be it on Instagram, TikTok or X.

Much of this information, where it concerns the Holocaust is false or misleading — some of it peddled by social media "influencers" who build their brands spreading conspiracy theories about Jews.

Social networks, we know, are generally subpar when it comes to moderating such content. Earlier this year, according to Forbes, "It took almost three days for X, to remove a post denying the Holocaust — and the move only came after the service received criticism from the Auschwitz Museum." (Research also shows that antisemitism spiked dramatically on X, in the aftermath of Elon Musk's takeover of the website.)

Holocaust denial is not new. What is new is the frequency with which young people come into contact with the false assertion and are swayed by it.

We hope Ontario's expanded education campaign can slow the spread.

Schools may see legal action for antisemitism

MARIE WOOLF OTTAWA

Lawyers are preparing legal action against schools and school boards across Canada that they say are failing to deal adequately with rising antisemitism, after a spike in abuse of Jewish children since the beginning of the war between Hamas and Israel.

Toronto personal injury lawyer Diamond and Diamond is working on around a dozen legal cases involving schools from B.C. to the Maritimes, as well as lawsuits against Toronto and Peel district school boards in Ontario.

Sandra Zisckind, managing partner at Diamond and Diamond, which is also preparing class-action lawsuits against universities, said: "I'm appalled and sickened that children cannot go to school and be who they are." She said that often the victim is blamed and moved out of the classroom by schools, rather than the perpetrator, but that the "lawsuits will hold them to task for what they do."

The Centre for Israel and Jewish Affairs has also set up a legal task force to help families, and says it has received an unprecedented number of reports of antisemitism in public schools since the conflict in the Mideast began last October.

They say elementary and high-school children have been punched, spat at, chased by groups of children shouting abuse, ostracized in class and faced antisemitic taunts – as well as Nazi salutes.

Tamara Gottlieb, founder of Fairness in Education, a task force designed to protect students and teachers from rising antisemitism and racism in schools, said she has been inundated with calls from Jewish teachers, parents and children, including those enduring chants of "we are going to finish the job that Hamas started – Jews must die."

She said many schools are not dealing with incidences adequately, and children and teachers have faced death threats.

"At one downtown [Toronto] school there was a little Jewish boy in the classroom, and there was a student who brought in a Nazi flag, playing Nazi music on his phone and encircled the Jewish boy, while playing the music," she said.

"And the Jewish boy got removed from the classroom after he broke the flag and the aggressor remained in the class."

The National Council of Canadian Muslims said that since October it had also "noted an exponential rise in Islamophobia and anti-Palestinian racism in schools across Canada."

"From students sharing experiences of violent harassment to bullying and silencing, there is a rise in hate, and schools need to be paying close attention," said NCCM education director Aasiyah Khan in an e-mail.

Aaron Kucharczuk, a Toronto parent, said antisemitism was now so prevalent that Jewish parents routinely exchange stories of their children's experiences. He said a neighbour's children were surrounded, kicked and hit by other children making comments about being "sent back to the gas chambers. And we're going to do to you what Hamas did to Israel."

Jaime Kirzner-Roberts, vice-president, GTA, Centre for Israel and Jewish Affairs, said it sometimes receives several dozen reports of antisemitism in schools in one day.

"These are reports of Jewish students subjected to slurs, bullying, and even assault; students finding their lockers covered routinely in swastikas or "free Palestine" graffiti; students told they should "die in a gas chamber," that they are "baby killers," or that they have no right to live in Canada," she said in an e-mail.

Twenty-seven universities have now replied to a letter sent in November by Liberal MPs, including Anthony Housefather, asking how they were dealing with antisemitism on campus.

"For me, the highlight is that all 27 confirmed that a call for the genocide of Jews violates their codes of conduct, irrespective of context," Mr. Housefather said in a statement Wednesday.

Toronto District School Board said it empathized with staff, students and their families over "increased incidences of antisemitism in our communities and schools."

"The TDSB takes all allegations of hate and racism very seriously and investigates the reports we receive. Each incident of hate or racism is addressed on a case-by-case basis, and can lead to disciplinary action including suspension and/or expulsion," Ryan Bird, a TDSB executive officer, said in a statement. He said it was making every effort to prevent hateful incidents from happening in the first place, including through education. Peel District School Board said in a statement that it "is deeply committed to nurturing inclusive and identity-affirming spaces where the diversity and humanity of all students, staff and communities are centred."

Former NDP chief says Jewish members feeling uncomfortable in the party

MARIE WOOLF OTTAWA

The former national director of the federal NDP says Jews are no longer feeling completely comfortable in the party, warning that this is a national problem for the New Democrats.

Nathan Rotman, who was also chief of staff to former Alberta premier Rachel Notley, made his remarks after former B.C. minister of postsecondary education Selina Robinson resigned from the province's NDP caucus, citing antisemitism by some of her colleagues.

Ms. Robinson, who is Jewish and will now sit as an independent, referred to antisemitism in the NDP caucus in a lengthy resignation letter Wednesday. She left her role as postsecondary education minister last month after an outcry from pro-Palestinian groups over a comment she made that Israel was founded on "a crappy piece of land."

In a post on the social-media platform X on Friday, Mr. Rotman, who is also Jewish, said "the letter by Robinson reflects the experiences of many in the NDP. This is not a BC problem, it's a national one. It's become more uncomfortable to be Jewish in the party and that's an understatement."

"I haven't left the party but it's certainly leaving me," he added.

Mr. Rotman declined a request from The Globe and Mail to elaborate on his comments.

The NDP has been vociferous in its support for Palestinians and pushed Prime Minister Justin Trudeau to back a ceasefire in the war between Hamas and Israel. NDP members have called for a halt to the selling of arms to Israel, and have been sharply critical of its bombing of Gaza.

Some NDP MPs, including Peter Julian, have also vocally condemned antisemitism, the rise of the far right and other forms of hate.

In her letter resigning from caucus, Ms. Robinson said the behaviour of some colleagues after the Hamas attacks on Israel "broke my heart."

"This is not the party I signed on with," she wrote. "It has become a party that is afraid to stand with people, people who are hurting. It is with all this in mind that I am leaving caucus to sit as an Independent."

The national director of the federal NDP, Lucy Watson, said it has been "a very difficult time for the Jewish community and the Palestinian community."

"We continue to build a Party that respects and values everyone and where democratic debate is welcome. Any time we hear that our members feel like we are falling short of that goal is an opportunity to reflect and resolve to do better," she said in a statement.

Richard Marceau, a former Bloc Québécois MP and general counsel of The Centre for Israel and Jewish Affairs, said "many progressive Jews – Jews who care deeply about social justice but are not willing to leave part of their identity at the door to enter the room – feel like the party has left them."

"What Selina Robinson's letter has done is shine a light on a problem with the NDP that we have raised alarms about for years," he said. The party has "been deaf to numerous attempts by people – both inside and outside the party – to seriously address" antisemitism.

B.C. Premier David Eby said Thursday that Ms. Robinson's resignation from the NDP caucus was "humbling," but he disagreed with Ms. Robinson's "characterization" of former colleagues she had accused of antisemitism in her letter, saying they "fight every day to fight racism and discrimination."

But Mr. Eby told journalists: "I have to accept as a leader, that as a Jewish woman with these unique experiences in our caucus, she didn't feel safe. She didn't feel safe with me to bring forward her concerns and she felt she had to resign. So I'll examine that."

THE GLOBE AND MAIL

ONTARIO EDITION ▪ FRIDAY, NOVEMBER 10, 2023 ▪ GLOBEANDMAIL.COM

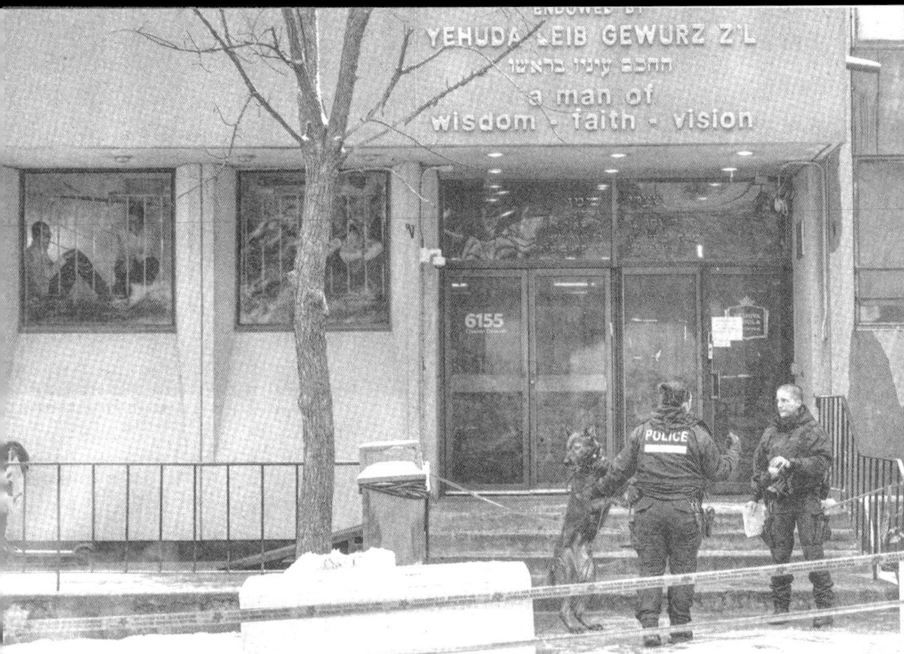

olice investigate outside Montreal's Yeshiva Gedola school, where a bullet hole was found Thursday morning. Another bullet mark, long with a shell casing, was discovered at the city's Azrieli Talmud Torah. RYAN REMIORZ/THE CANADIAN PRESS

ewish communities shaken by spike in hate incidents since Mideast war's onset

RÉDÉRIK-XAVIER DUHAMEL MONTREAL
IKE HAGER VANCOUVER
INDSAY JONES HALIFAX

wo empty Montreal Jewish schools hit by unfire, Molotov cocktails ignited at a synagogue and the headquarters of a Jewish on-profit – four hate incidents this week n the city that have brought a new level of nxiety to Jewish communities across Canada.

Montreal has seen a surge in hate-crime ases since the Oct. 7 Hamas attack on srael, with police adding the most recent ncidents to a list of another 41 targeting ewish people and 14 targeting Arab-Musim communities.

The numbers far outpace the usual rate hat Montreal's residents report hate ncidents, with investigators opening 238 ch cases last year, according to Statistics Canada.

Up until this week, police across Canada had mostly reported non-violent hate incidents, as the Israel-Hamas war inflames long-standing tensions that cut across religious, ethnic and ideological lines. Large, mostly pro-Palestinian demonstrations are being regularly held in multiple cities across Canada, with political leaders calling for calm and police ramping up patrols in affected communities.

Jean-Pierre Brabant, a spokesperson for the Montreal police, said that on Thursday morning, school staff found at least one bullet hole and a shell casing at a Jewish school in the Côte-des-Neiges neighbourhood, and a bullet hole at a school in Outremont.

Megan Saleh said she pulled her daughter out of class early at Azrieli Talmud Torah in Côte-des-Neiges, because she, like many other parents, was worried her child would be scared.

"I think that the antisemitism that's growing is awful, and bigger organizations – government, schools, universities – they need to condemn violence of all forms," she said. "This is a kids' school, it's too much."

Federation CJA, a Montreal-based Jewish advocacy organization, said Thursday that it has requested an increased police presence after the school shootings, one of which occurred at Yeshiva Gedola. The group also said it will fund increased security around other institutions after a Molotov cocktail was lit at its offices Tuesday as well as at a local synagogue.

"We understand that this adds stress and anxiety to our community members," the federation said in a statement. "We urge you to continue to take part in Jewish life while remaining extremely vigilant."

▪ ANTISEMITISM, A3

SUN COMMENT

If it's not about Jews, stop targeting them

From the moment protests in Canada against Israel began in the wake of Hamas' terrorist attack on Oct. 7, protesters have insisted their protests are against Israel, not Jews.

This while many "protesters" vandalize businesses owned by Jews and demonstrate outside restaurants owned by Jews and gathering places frequented by Jews.

That's to say nothing of others "protesting" by firebombing a synagogue and a community centre, firing bullets at Jewish schools, painting Swastikas on synagogues and targeting Jewish homes by smearing then with Swastikas and other Nazi graffiti.

Federal Liberal MP Marco Mendicino, who represents Toronto's Eglinton-Lawrence riding, which has a significant Jewish population, recently denounced repeated anti-Israel protests on a highway overpass in his community, described by one of the protesters as a "Zionist-infested area."

Where they're protesting is within walking distance of two synagogues and as Mendicino rightly said on X — "Those who call the Avenue Rd. & (Hwy.) 401 a 'Zionist Infested Area' betray their clearly Anti-Semitic intent to incite hatred towards a Jewish neighbourhood. This is unacceptable."

As Mendicino noted: "It is against the Criminal Code to promote hate (s.319), obstruct a highway (s.423), cause a disturbance (s.175), or cause mischief (s.430). When these laws aren't enforced, it emboldens more law breaking, and undermines public safety.

"Anti-Semitism no longer merely lurks in the shadows. It is now increasingly in plain sight."

Because anti-Semitism is now in plain sight, Toronto Police established a command centre outside another Jewish day school in the same riding days after the Oct. 7 attack, and have been there ever since, while a cruiser is assigned 24/7outside a Jewish home for the aged on the same street a short drive away.

No form of this hatred — whether targeted against Jews, Muslims, Arabs or Palestinians in Canada — should be tolerated anywhere in this country.

Protesters have every right to demonstrate against the loss of Palestinian lives caused by Israel's military response to Hamas' attack and there are plenty of places to protest that don't imply threats against Jews.

Targeting Jewish-owned businesses, schools, places of worship and neighbourhoods — as if Jews in Canada are responsible for Israel's policies — is classic Jew hatred.

Appeasing it will only cause it to spread.

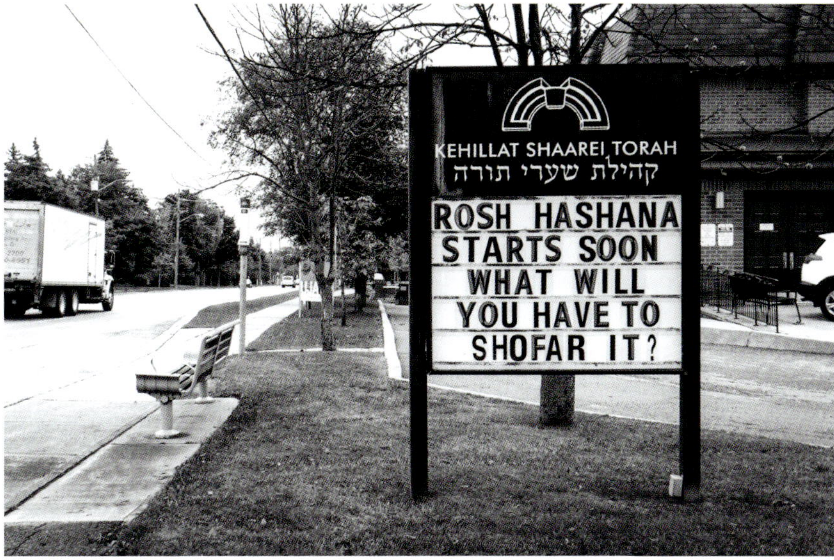
KEHILLAT SHAAREI TORAH
קהילת שערי תורה
ROSH HASHANA
STARTS SOON
WHAT WILL
YOU HAVE TO
SHOFAR IT?

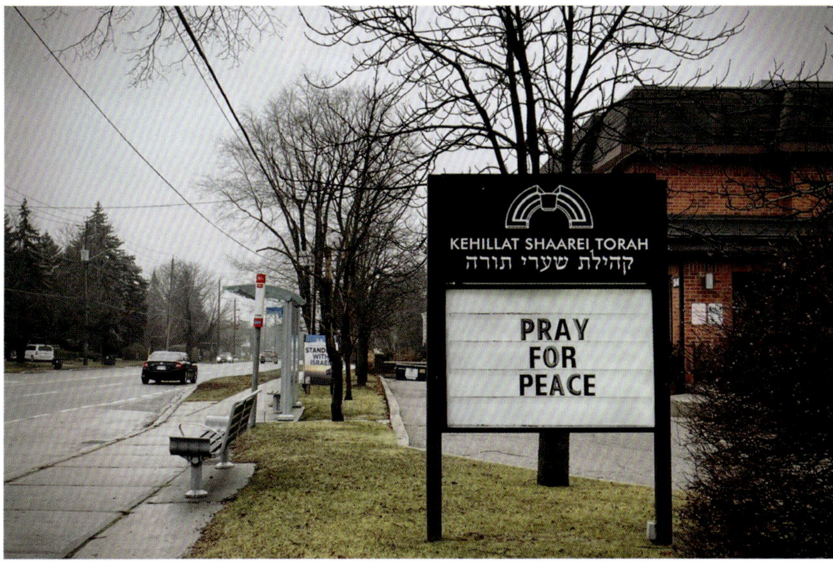
KEHILLAT SHAAREI TORAH
קהילת שערי תורה
PRAY
FOR
PEACE

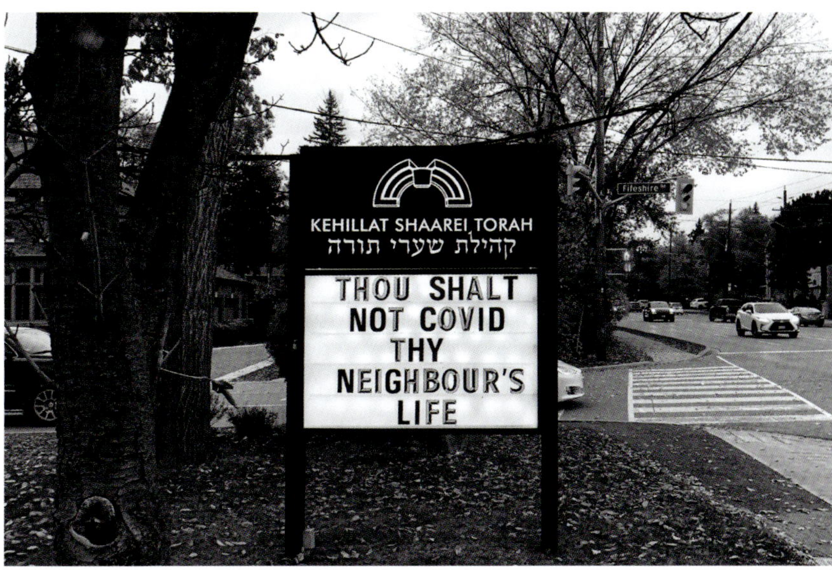
KEHILLAT SHAAREI TORAH
קהילת שערי תורה
THOU SHALT
NOT COVID
THY
NEIGHBOUR'S
LIFE
Fifeshire

Friends of Simon Wiesenthal Center
@CanadianFSWC

A masked individual was caught on camera smashing windows with a hammer at Kehillat Shaarei Torah in Toronto.

We denounce this heinous act of violence targeting a Jewish place of worship.

@TorontoPolice Hate Crime Unit is investigating.

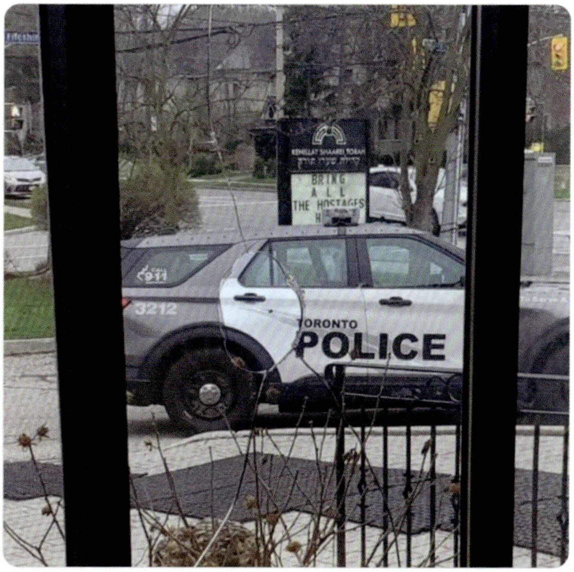

3:03 PM · Apr 19, 2024 · **856** Views

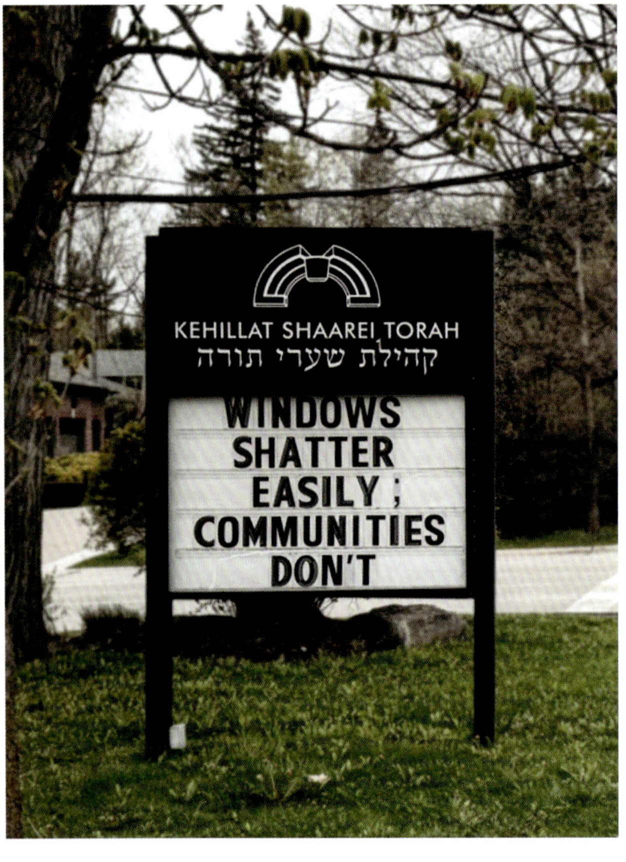
KEHILLAT SHAAREI TORAH
קהילת שערי תורה
WINDOWS
SHATTER
EASILY ;
COMMUNITIES
DON'T

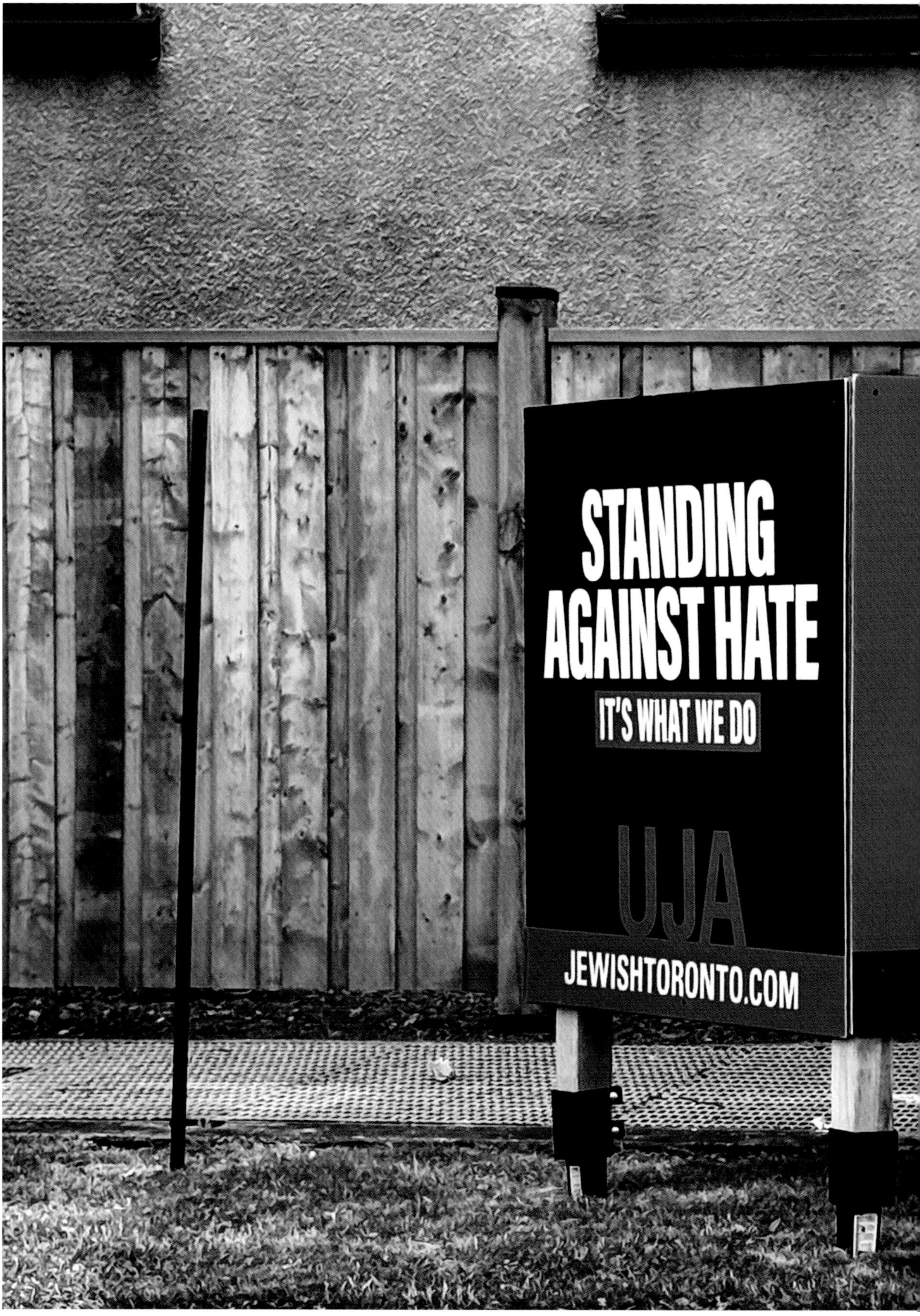
STANDING
AGAINST HATE
IT'S WHAT WE DO
UJA
JEWISHTORONTO.COM

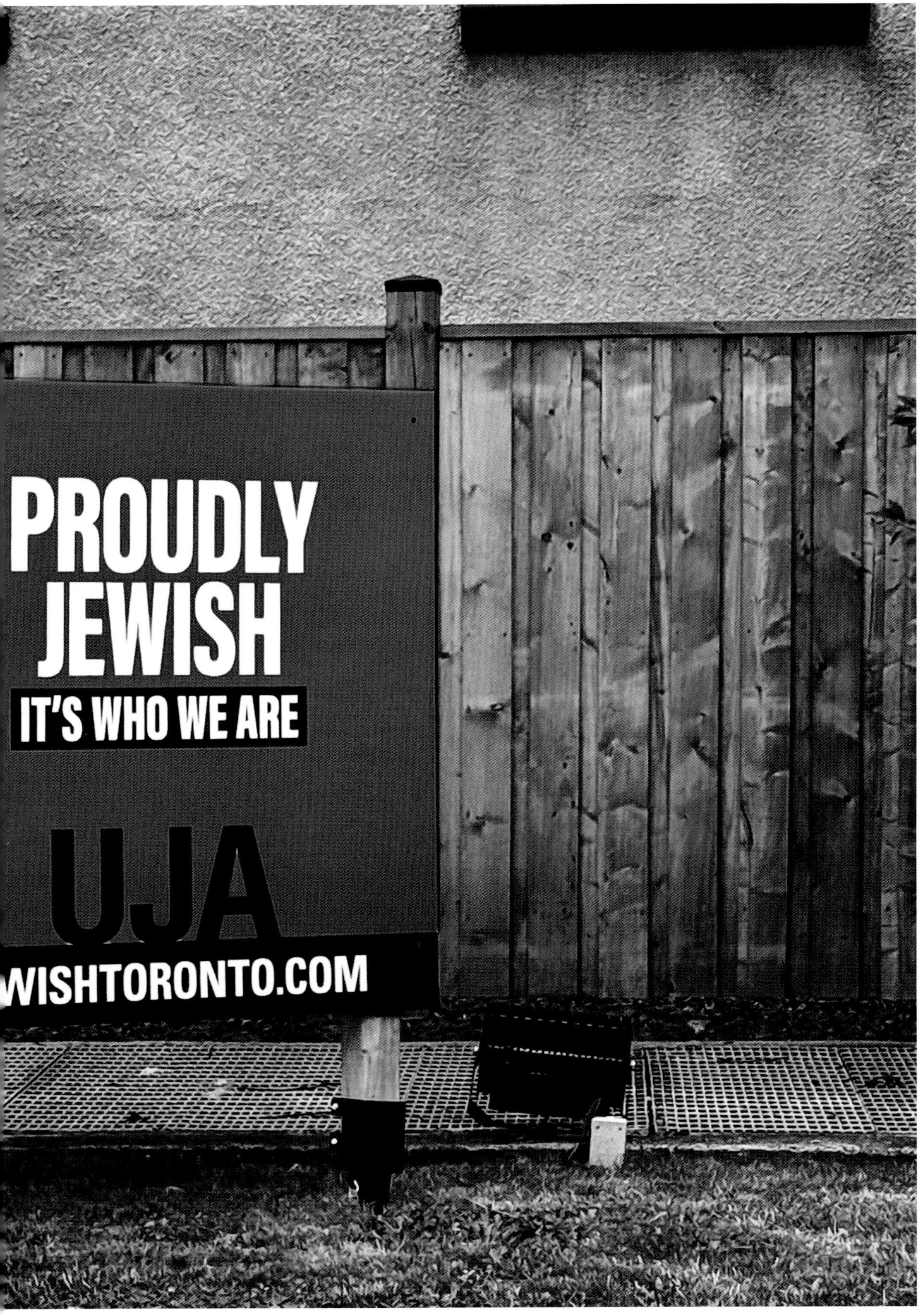
PROUDLY
JEWISH
IT'S WHO WE ARE
UJA
WISHTORONTO.COM

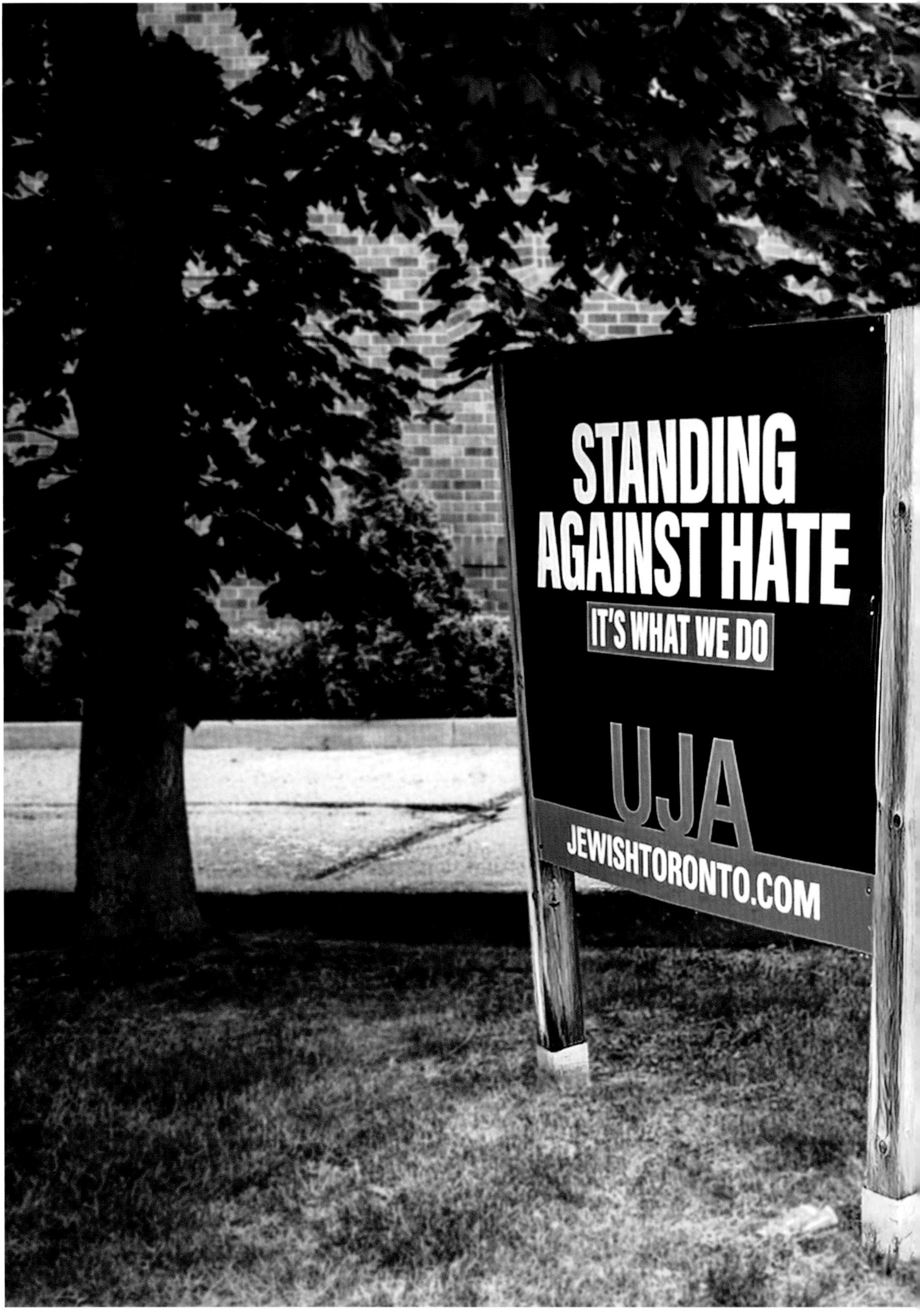
STANDING
AGAINST HATE
IT'S WHAT WE DO
UJA
JEWISHTORONTO.COM

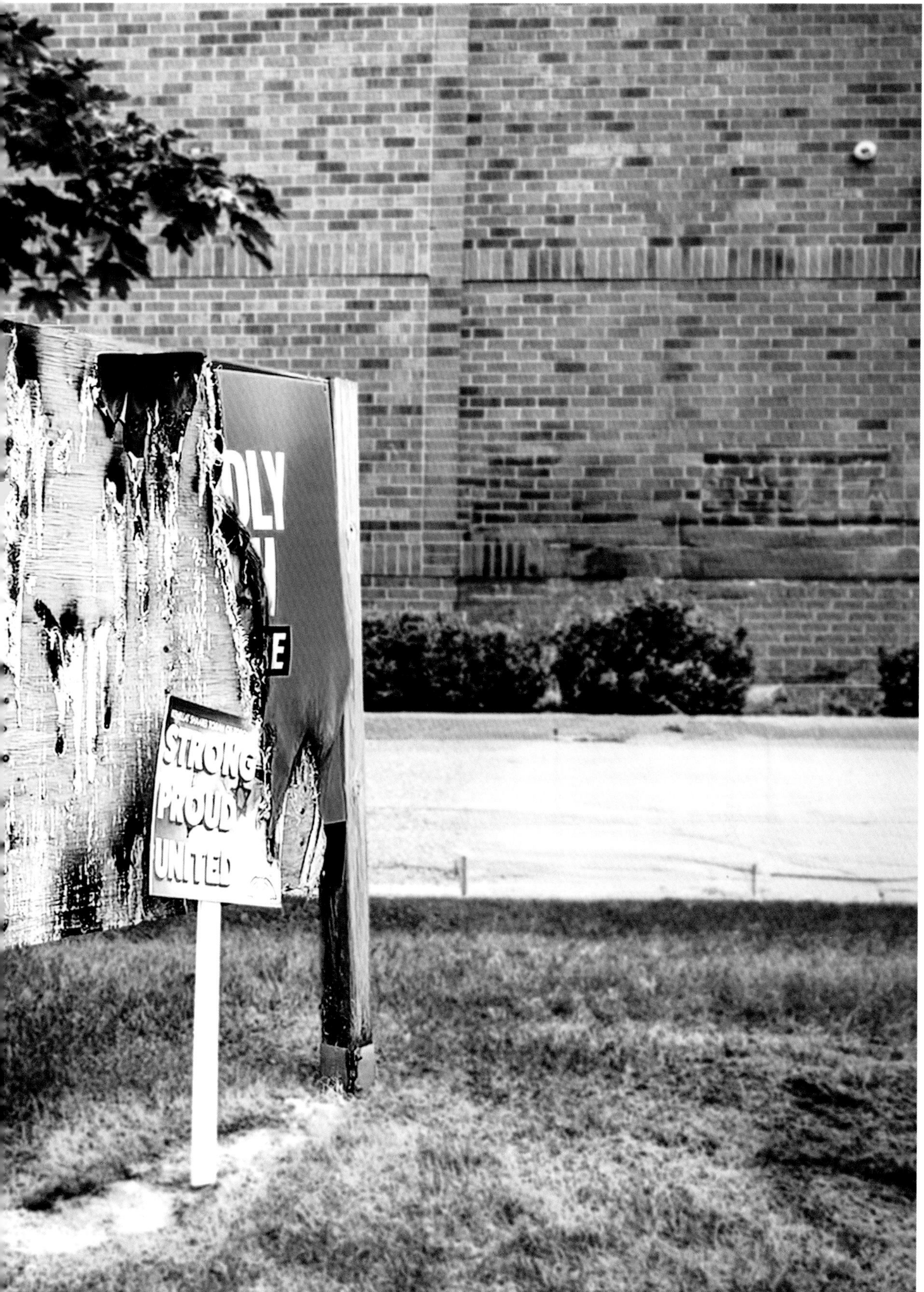
STRONG
PROUD
UNITED

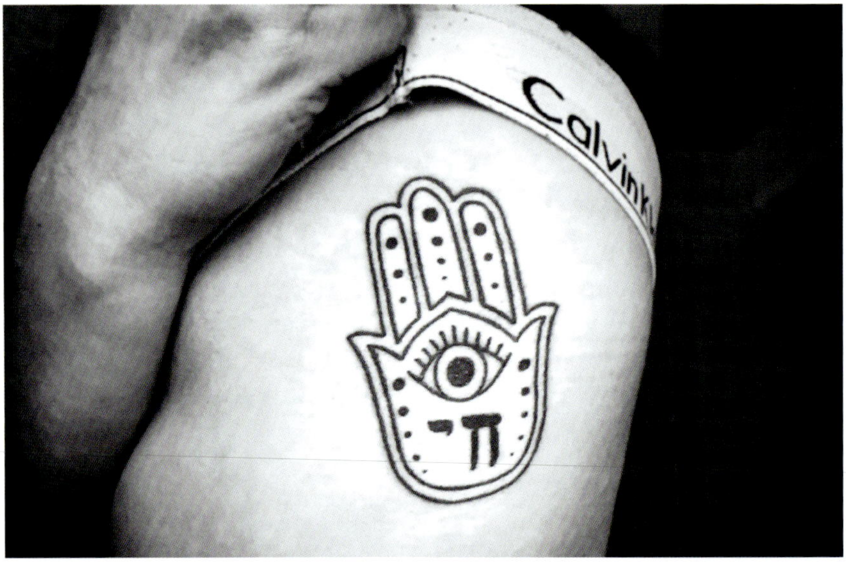
חי

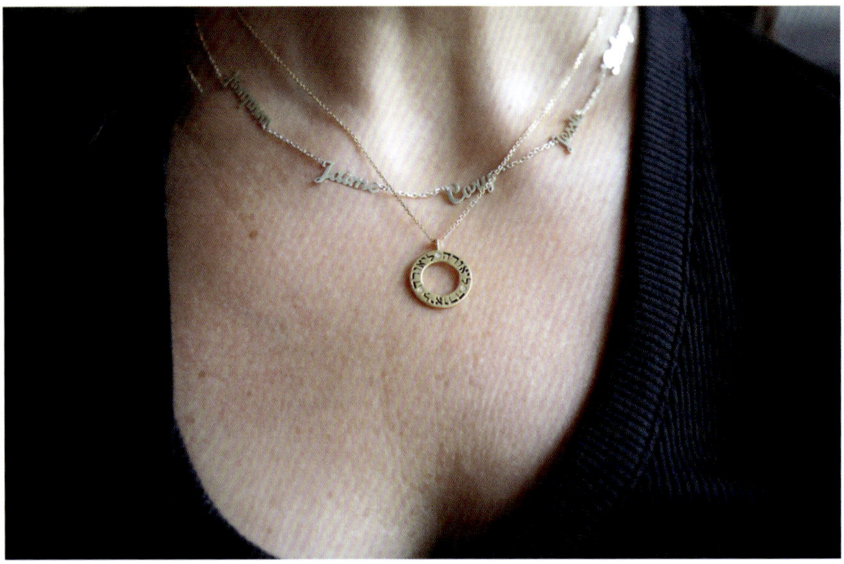

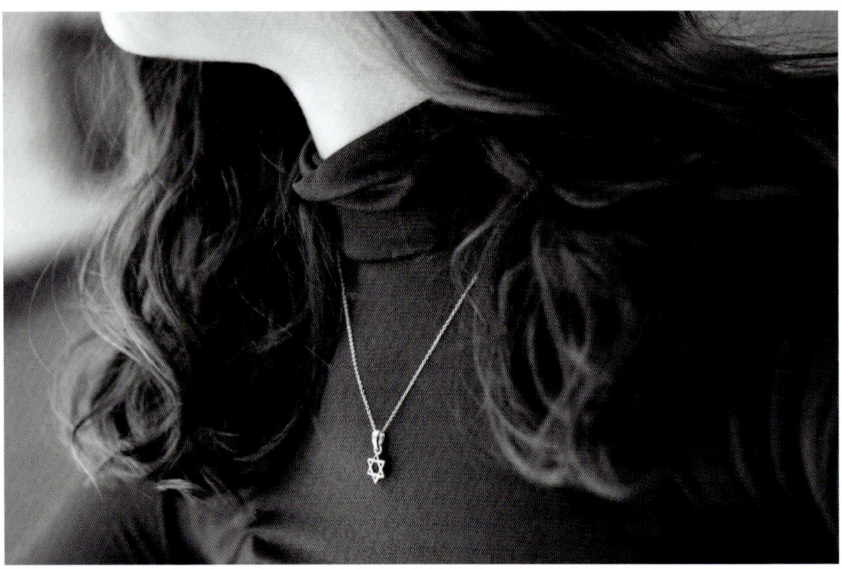

I think the more persecution that is happening towards Jews, the more Jewish I feel. I think that's part of a don't-fuck-with-me attitude.

It just makes me not only tighter with my community, tighter with the Jewish community, but it makes me want to be more proud of being Jewish. Because being Black, you can't hide it.

I feel more and more affiliated with people who are as equally embattled as I am, as I feel. There are people who are like me; who are being targeted just because they are like me.

I wear a Star of David around my neck, and I'm proud of it. I'm not going to hide who I am as a Jew, because I don't think anybody should have to hide who they are, what they practice, or how they believe. We've come too far for that.

I don't belong to any shul (synagogue), or belong to any organization, but I still try to immerse myself from time to time. I guess I would say I'm part of the Hillel organization, but being trans and Jewish I mainly go to the LGBTQ Jewish events within Hillel.

In every culture we've lived in for, you know, 2,000 years, we have also kept the community together through ritual. I have to say above all through Torah, because even today I can go anywhere in the world, and I could have done so at any time in history, and no matter what Jewish culture I belonged to I could identify with Jews anywhere in the world through Torah.

I think you're going to want to do it [carry on traditions] as you grow up. And even if you don't do it in your young adult years, as soon as you become a parent, all of a sudden upon you is the responsibility to pass that onto your kids.

So, in a way, that kind of traditional critical thinking and engaging with the Jewish holidays draws me in. And I think it draws my son in.

I think that because Jews have always been a diaspora, the only way to maintain our Jewishness is to maintain the holidays that are so important to all of us. Because it's so easy to lose your identity.

And it's important to know when you're standing on Rosh Hashana and they're blowing the shofar that it's being blown in every synagogue throughout the world. And I find that very touching.

There is the sense of belonging to a greater thing than you. And over time, I think even if you are kind of thickheaded, you realize that Jewish history and Jewish life is greater than you. And that it's good to belong.

I think it might be fair to say that Jews are in some aspect very chameleonic. We've adapted to every culture that we've lived in.

It's the traditions and the oral history that pass down from generation to generation. The only thing that actually distinguishes people as a group is how they practice those events in their lives. Because day to day, everybody does the same things. Everybody works, everybody eats meals, everybody goes to sleep, everybody showers.

I have four grandchildren, and we've had namings in the synagogue. Neither set of parents is remotely observant, but these kids have all been kind of blessed and welcomed by my rabbi, whom I love. And it's just there. The ground is set, the seeds are planted, and I don't think a lot can grow if you haven't planted some seeds first.

It's tough to say how important it is to me that we do Shabbat or whatever, because to me it's an opportunity to see family, which is important. The ritual of it doesn't really have any impact on my day-to-day life, but it's important to me that someone in my family is organizing it. Because I think that it's important to continue.

I think [Jews] feel that this is something that's been done for centuries. And even though they may not believe in the root of it, they believe in the tradition, and it's really something that binds people together. And so when you consider the table with Jews from all different walks of life—different practices, some Orthodox, some not—and I can have a conversation about Judaism or about a specific tradition, I think it really goes to show the Jewish community binds you together more than just the religious element of it.

The rituals signify the things that are really strong, and they carry you through. Those are the big memories you have in your lives. I have memories of gathering with people and, like, literally breaking bread. So the traditions and the songs and certain foods, and a certain effort you make, I think those things are really important. And for me it's not necessarily about God, but it's about your cultural identity and showing up.

I think that adversity is what makes us stronger and what brings us all together regardless of where we are in the world. And I think that's why we continue to have these traditions and holidays and gatherings that are important to all of us, regardless of our religious affiliation. Again, it's so much more than just a religion, and it needs to be because that's how we survive.

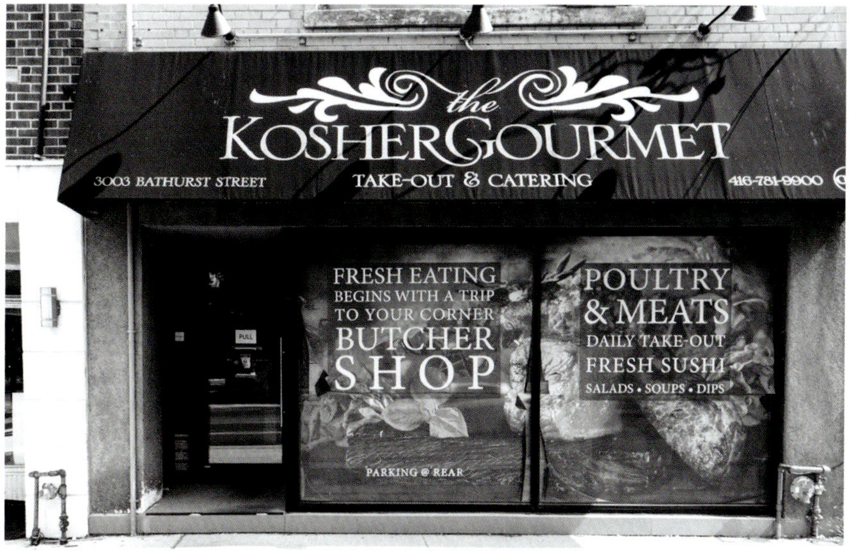
the
KOSHER GOURMET
3003 BATHURST STREET
TAKE-OUT & CATERING
FRESH EATING
BEGINS WITH A TRIP
TO YOUR CORNER
BUTCHER
SHOP
POULTRY
& MEATS
DAILY TAKE-OUT
FRESH SUSHI
SALADS • SOUPS • DIPS
PARKING @ REAR

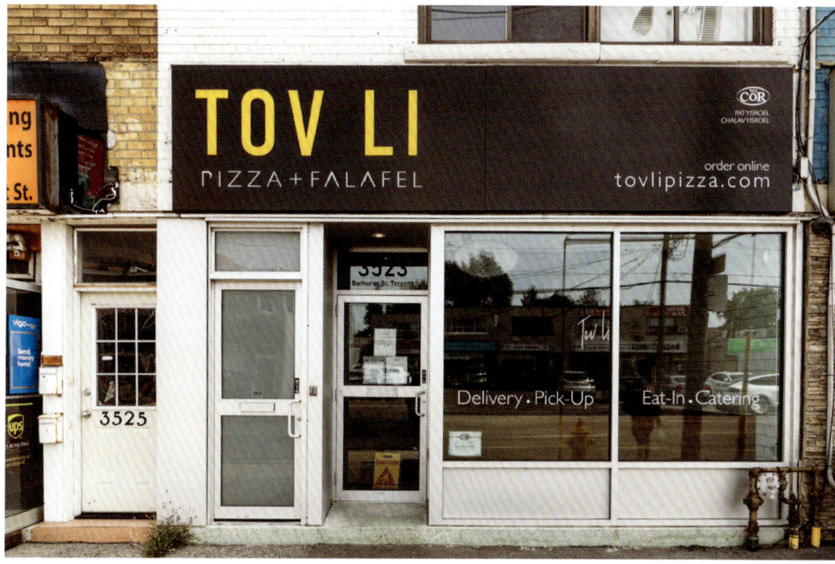
TOV LI
PIZZA+FALAFEL
order online
tovlipizza.com
3525
Delivery . Pick-Up
Eat-In . Catering

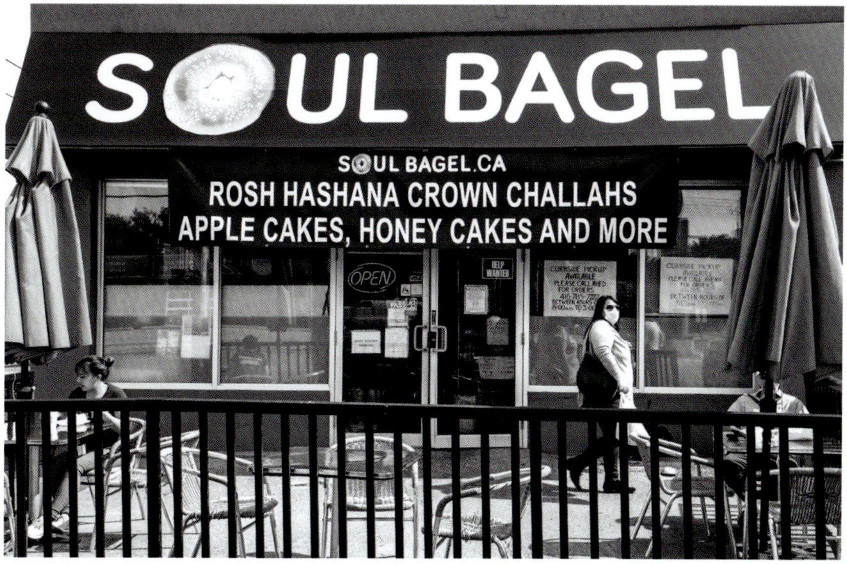
SOUL BAGEL
SOUL BAGEL.CA
ROSH HASHANA CROWN CHALLAHS
APPLE CAKES, HONEY CAKES AND MORE
OPEN

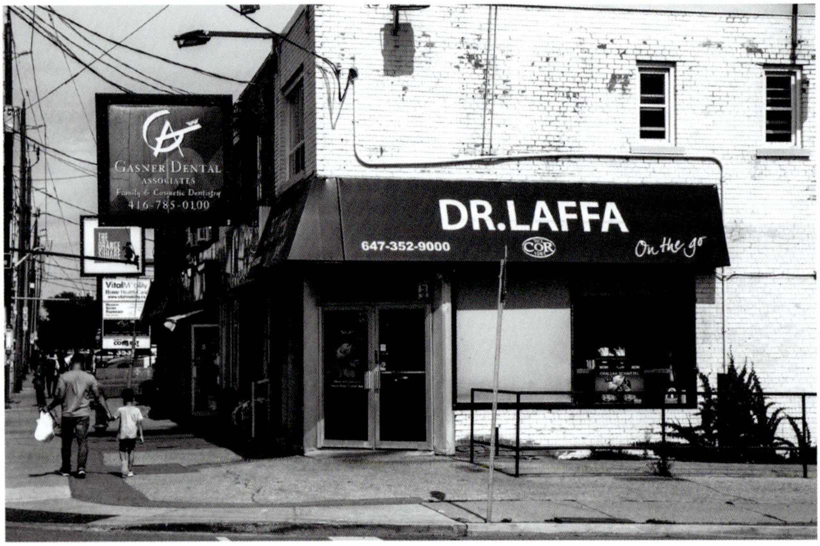
GASNER DENTAL
ASSOCIATES
Family & Cosmetic Dentistry
416-785-0100
DR.LAFFA
647-352-9000
COR
On the go

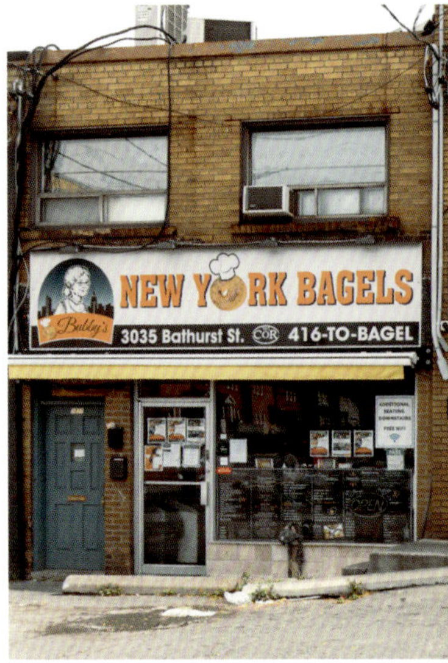
NEW YORK BAGELS
Bubby's
3035 Bathurst St.
COR
416-TO-BAGEL

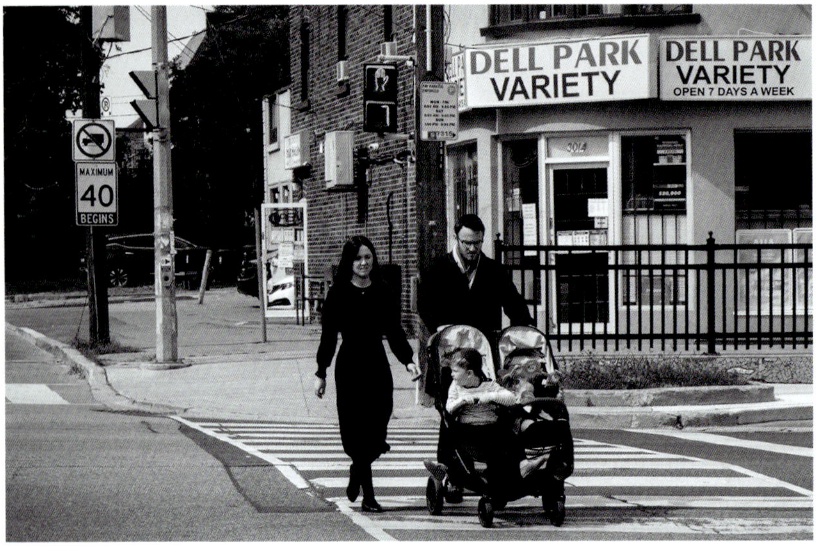
DELL PARK
VARIETY
DELL PARK
VARIETY
OPEN 7 DAYS A WEEK
MAXIMUM
40
BEGINS
3014

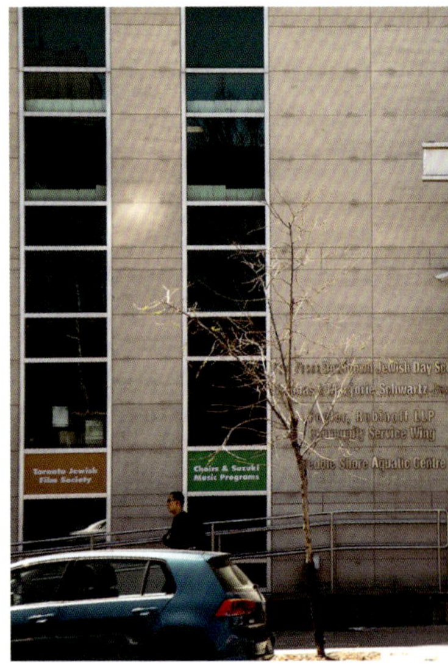
Toronto Jewish
Film Society
Choirs & Suzuki
Music Programs

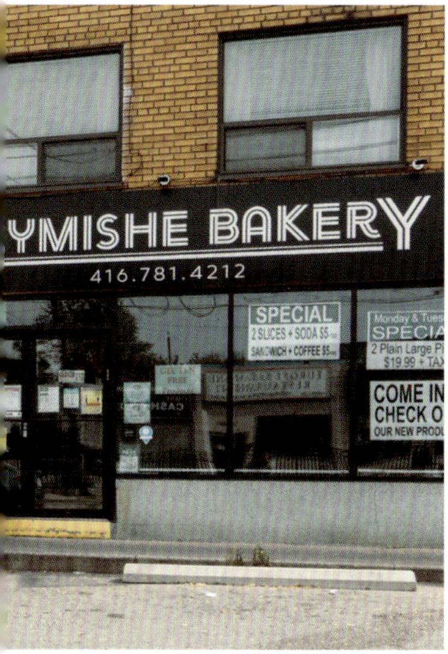
YMISHE BAKERY
416.781.4212
SPECIAL
2 SLICES + SODA $5
SANDWICH + COFFEE $5
Monday & Tues
SPECIA
2 Plain Large Pi
$19.99 + TAX
COME IN
CHECK O
OUR NEW PRODU

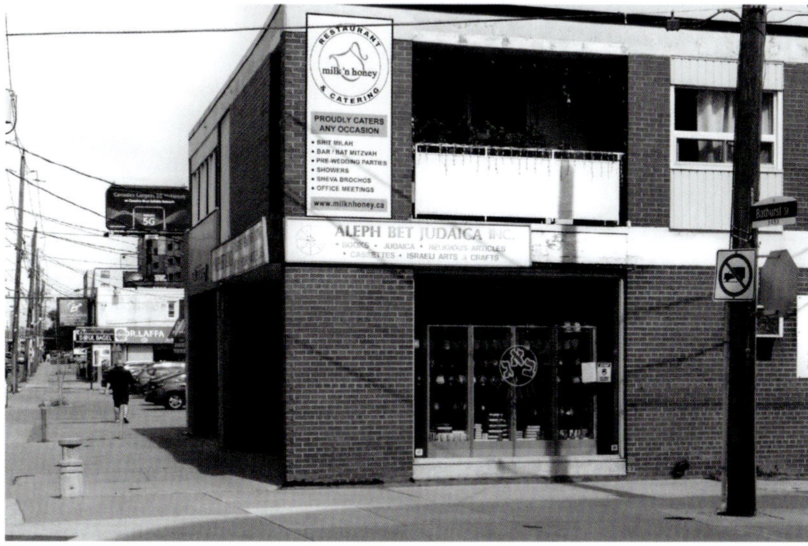
RESTAURANT
milk'n honey
& CATERING
PROUDLY CATERS
ANY OCCASION
• BRIT MILAH
• BAR / BAT MITZVAH
• PRE-WEDDING PARTIES
• SHOWERS
• SHEVA BROCHOS
• OFFICE MEETINGS
www.milknhoney.ca
ALEPH BET JUDAICA INC.
• BOOKS • JUDAICA • RELIGIOUS ARTICLES
• CASSETTES • ISRAELI ARTS & CRAFTS
Bathurst St
5G
DR.LAFFA

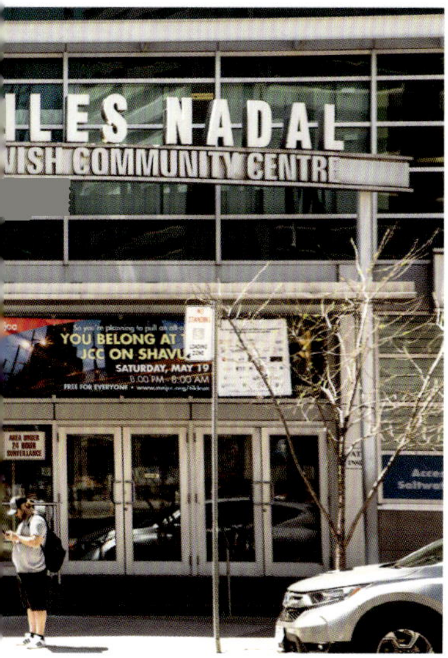
ILES NADAL
VISH COMMUNITY CENTRE
YOU BELONG AT
JCC ON SHAVU
SATURDAY, MAY 19
8:00 PM - 6:00 AM
AREA UNDER 24 HOUR SURVEILLANCE

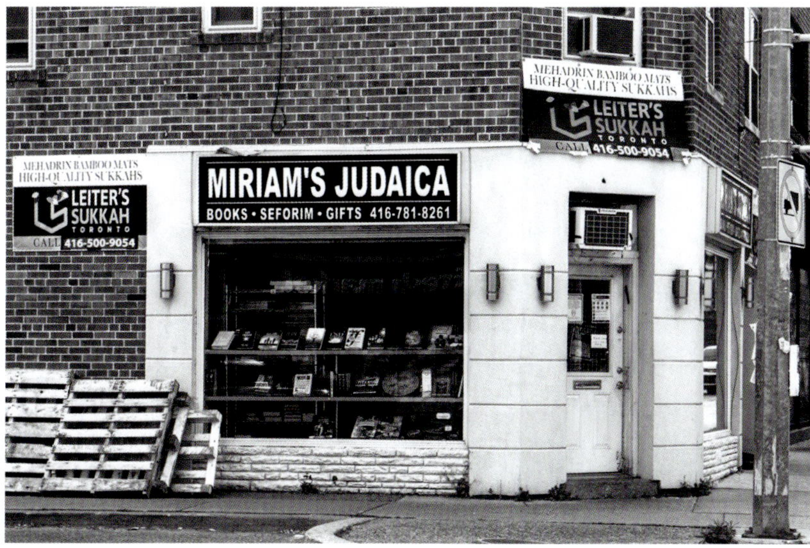
MEHADRIN BAMBOO MATS
HIGH-QUALITY SUKKAHS
LEITER'S
SUKKAH
TORONTO
CALL 416-500-9054
MIRIAM'S JUDAICA
BOOKS • SEFORIM • GIFTS 416-781-8261
MEHADRIN BAMBOO MATS
HIGH-QUALITY SUKKAHS
LEITER'S
SUKKAH
TORONTO
CALL 416-500-9054

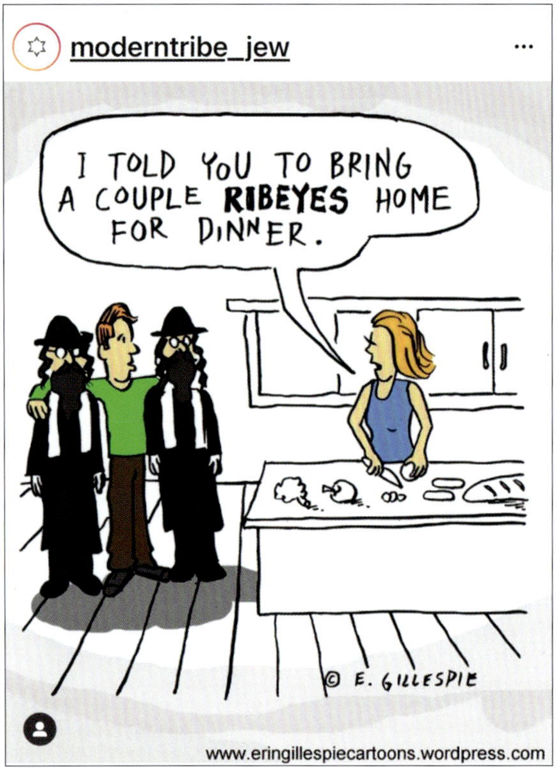
moderntribe_jew
I TOLD YOU TO BRING A COUPLE RIBEYES HOME FOR DINNER.
© E. GILLESPIE
www.eringillespiecartoons.wordpress.com

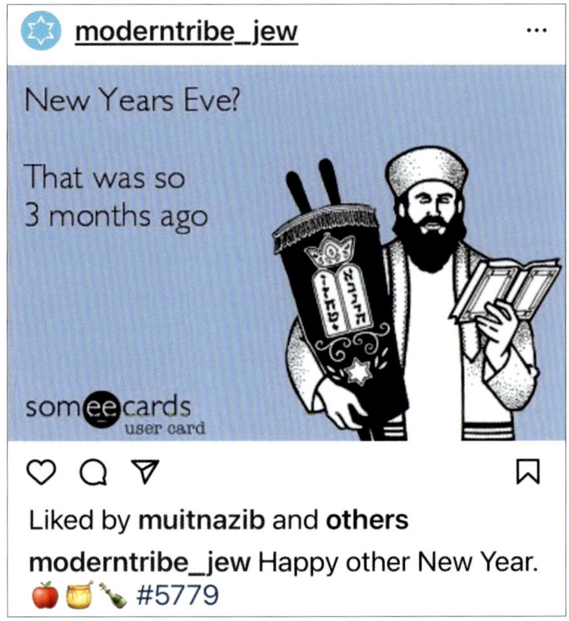
moderntribe_jew
New Years Eve?
That was so 3 months ago
someecards user card
Liked by muitnazib and others
moderntribe_jew Happy other New Year. 🍎🍯🍾 #5779

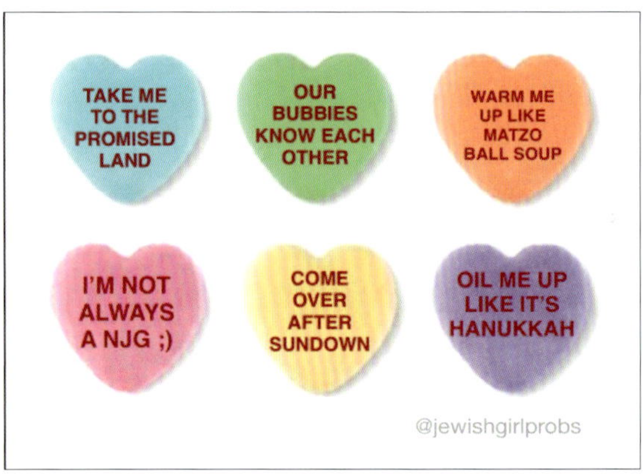
TAKE ME TO THE PROMISED LAND
OUR BUBBIES KNOW EACH OTHER
WARM ME UP LIKE MATZO BALL SOUP
I'M NOT ALWAYS A NJG ;)
COME OVER AFTER SUNDOWN
OIL ME UP LIKE IT'S HANUKKAH
@jewishgirlprobs

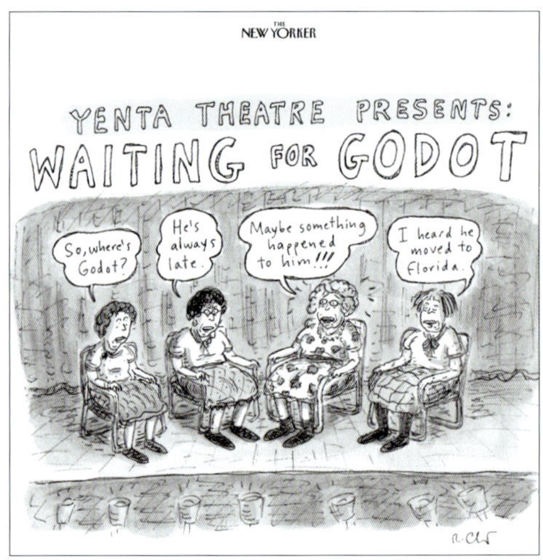
THE NEW YORKER
YENTA THEATRE PRESENTS:
WAITING FOR GODOT
So, where's Godot?
He's always late.
Maybe something happened to him!!!
I heard he moved to Florida.

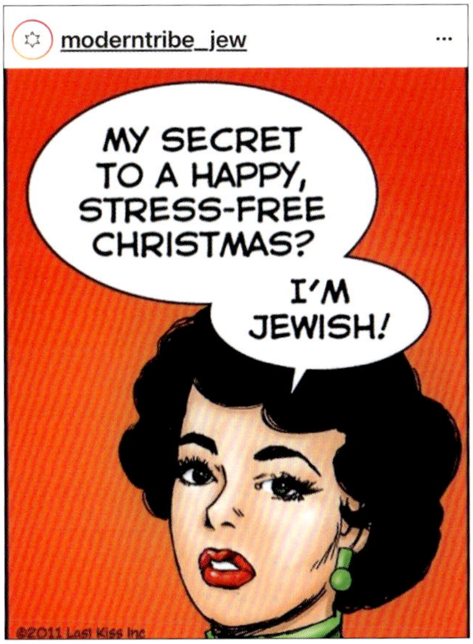

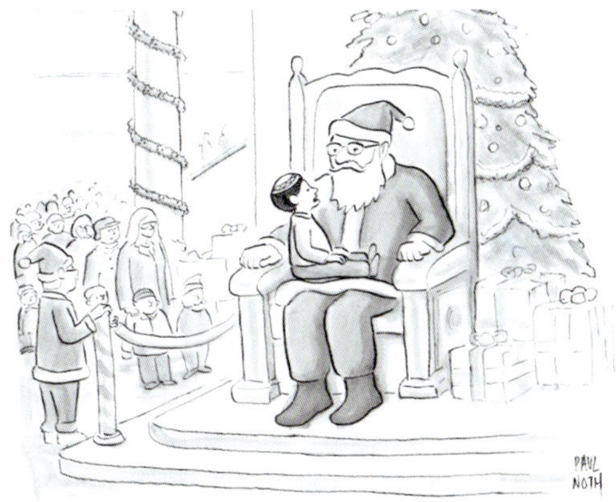

"First of all, this conversation never happened."

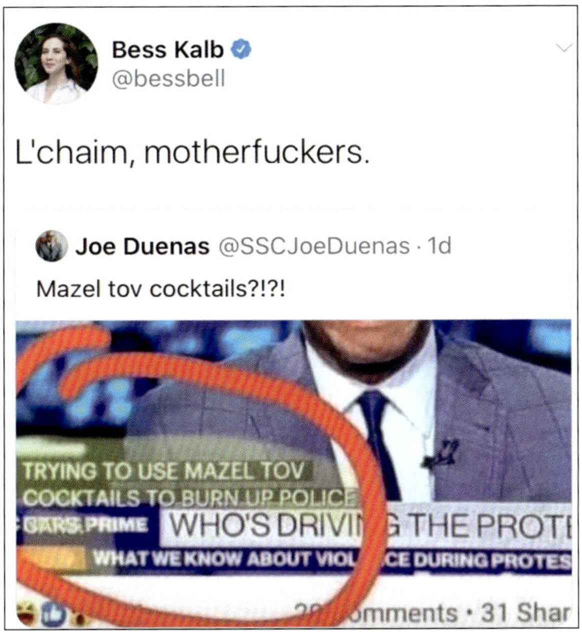

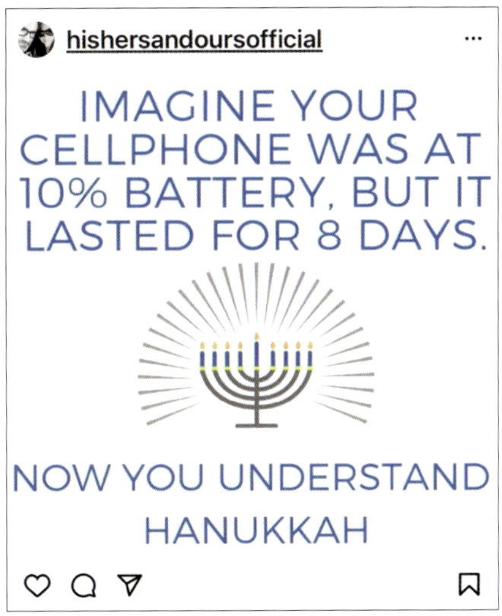

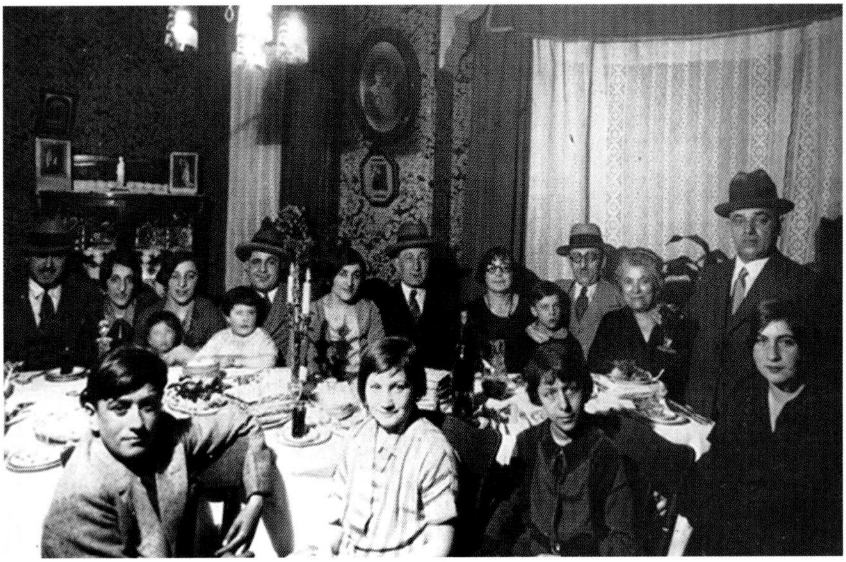

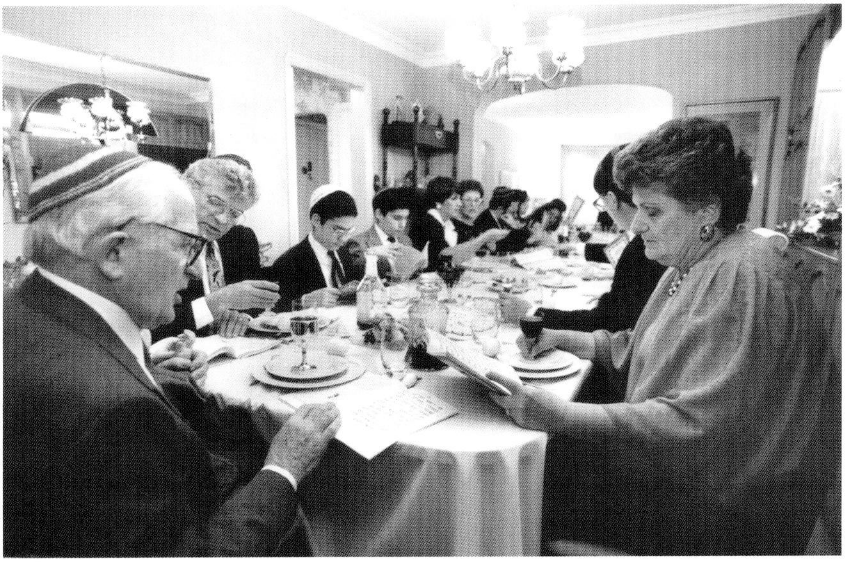

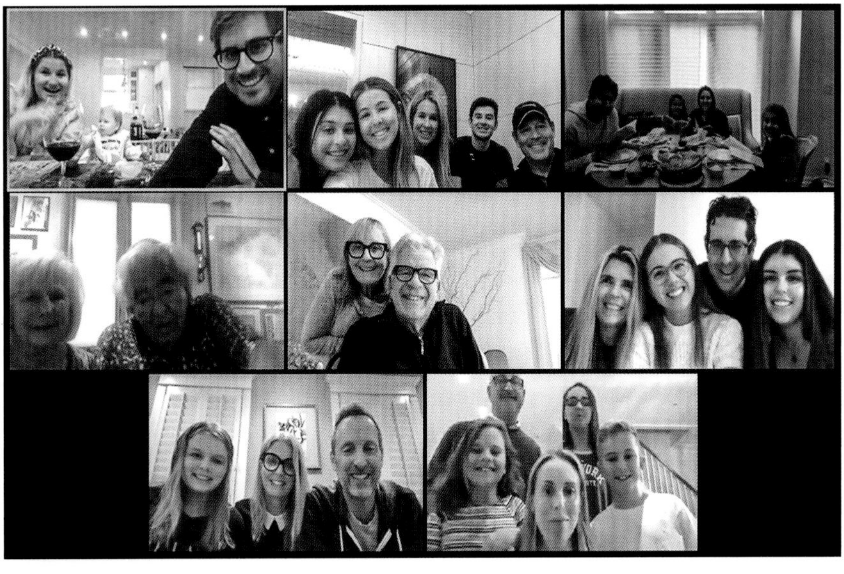

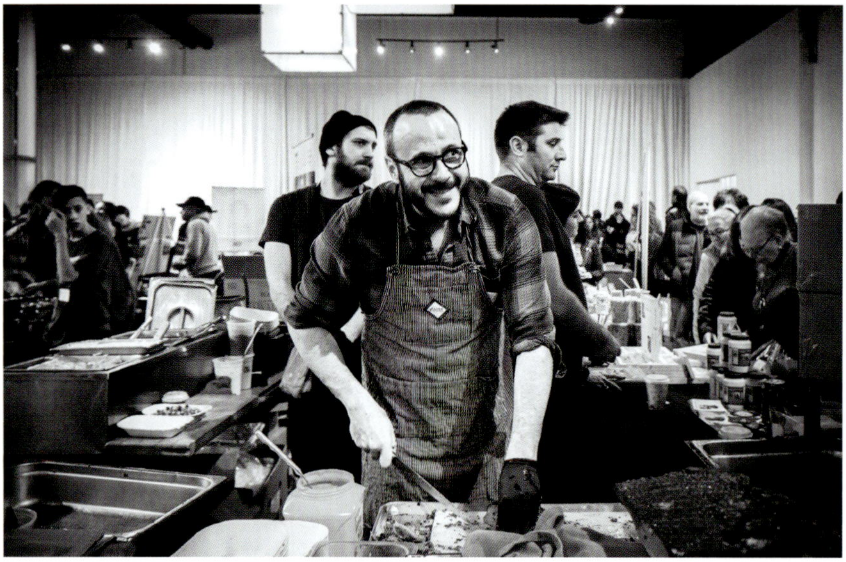

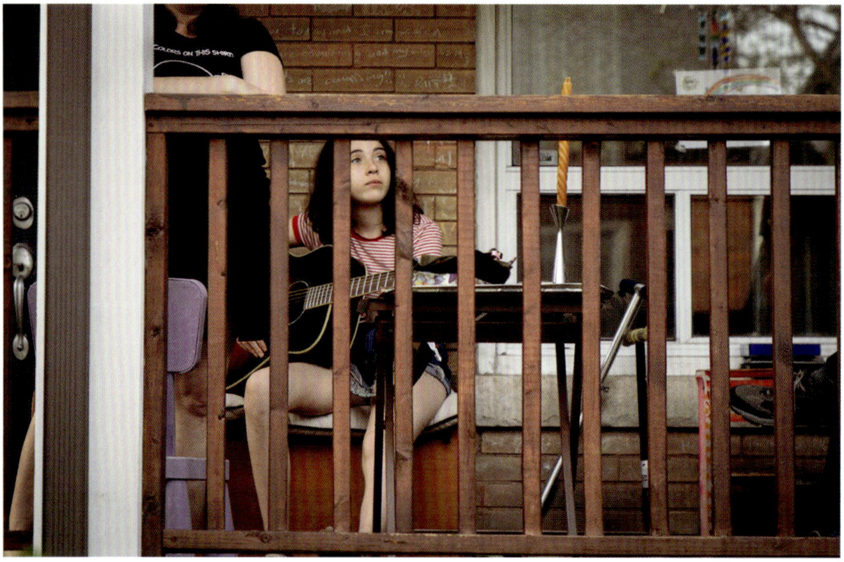

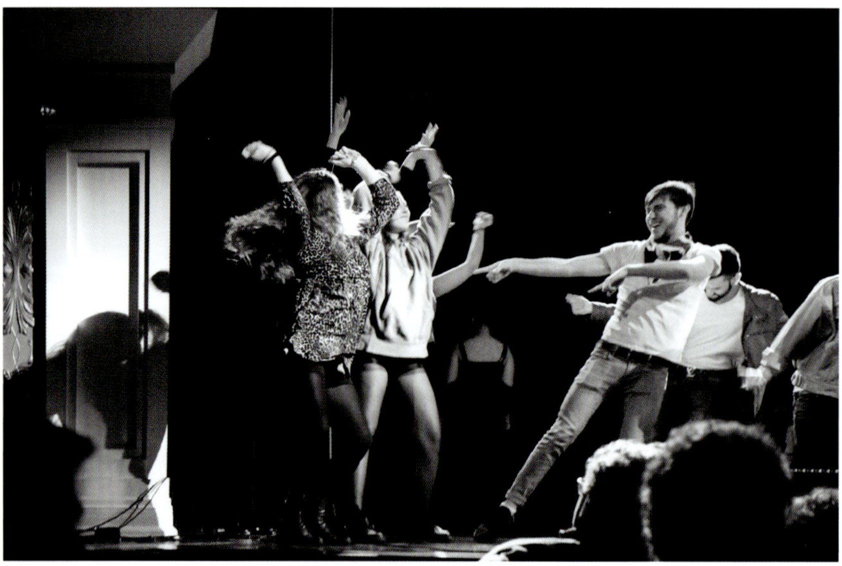

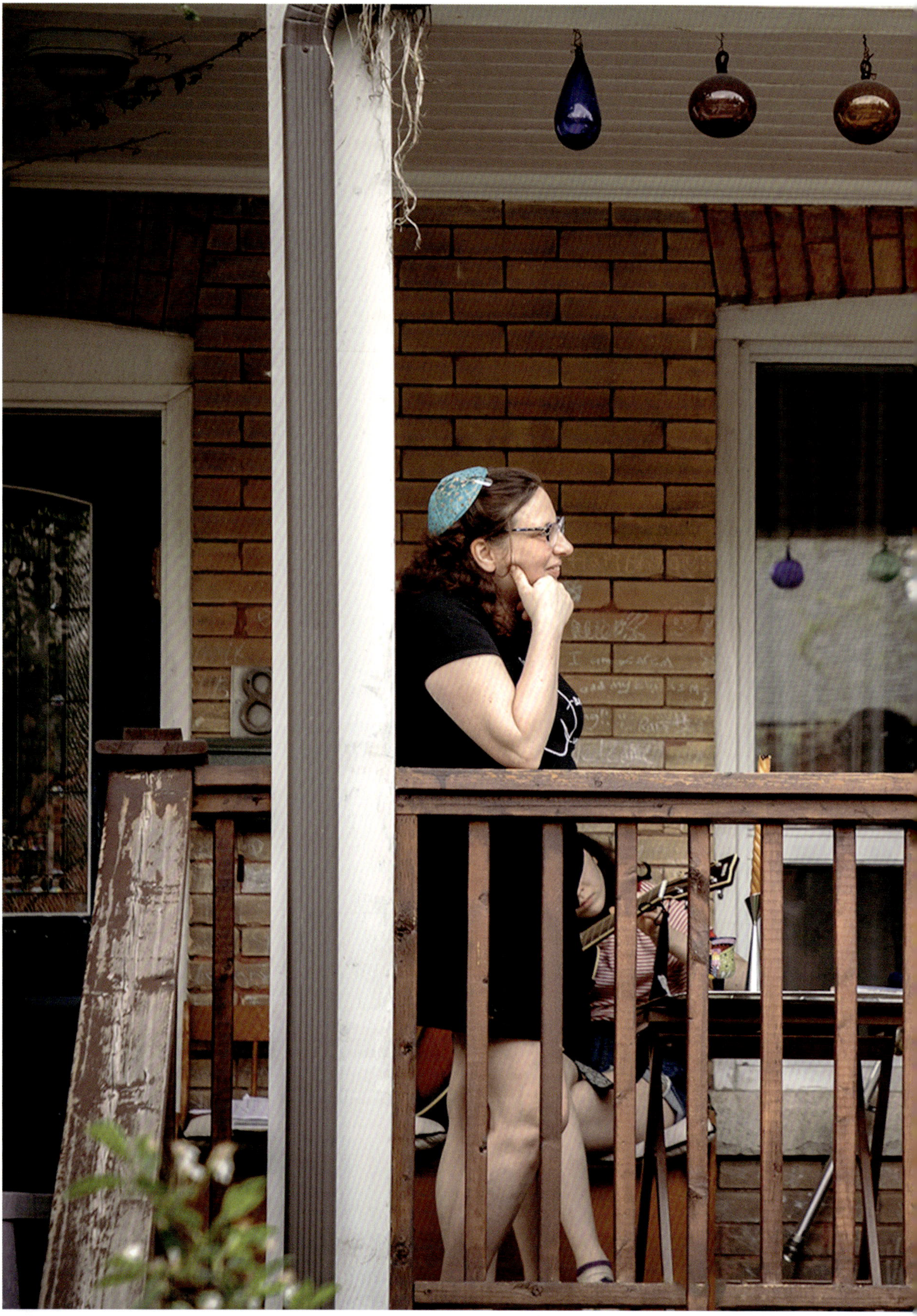
8

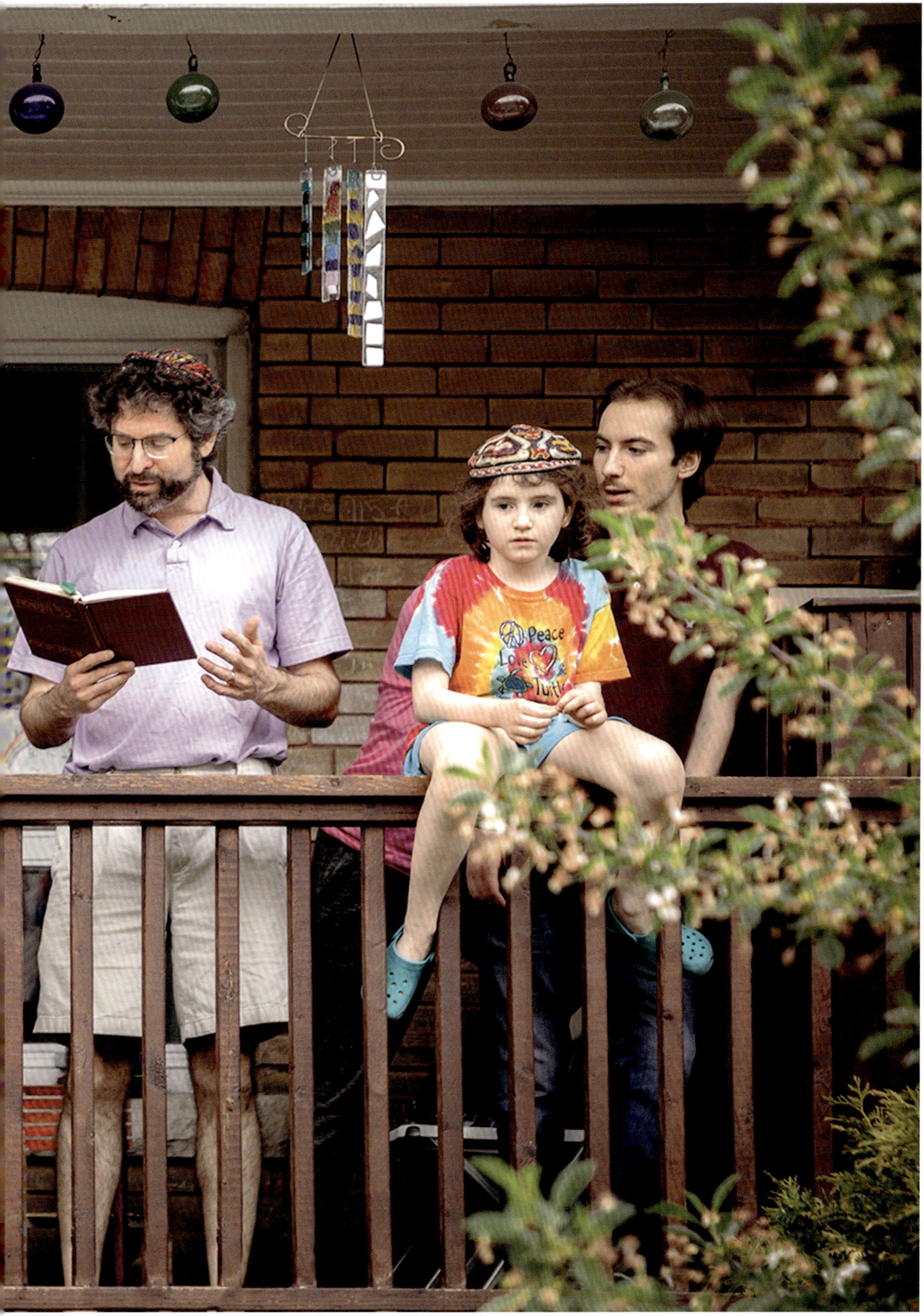
Peace

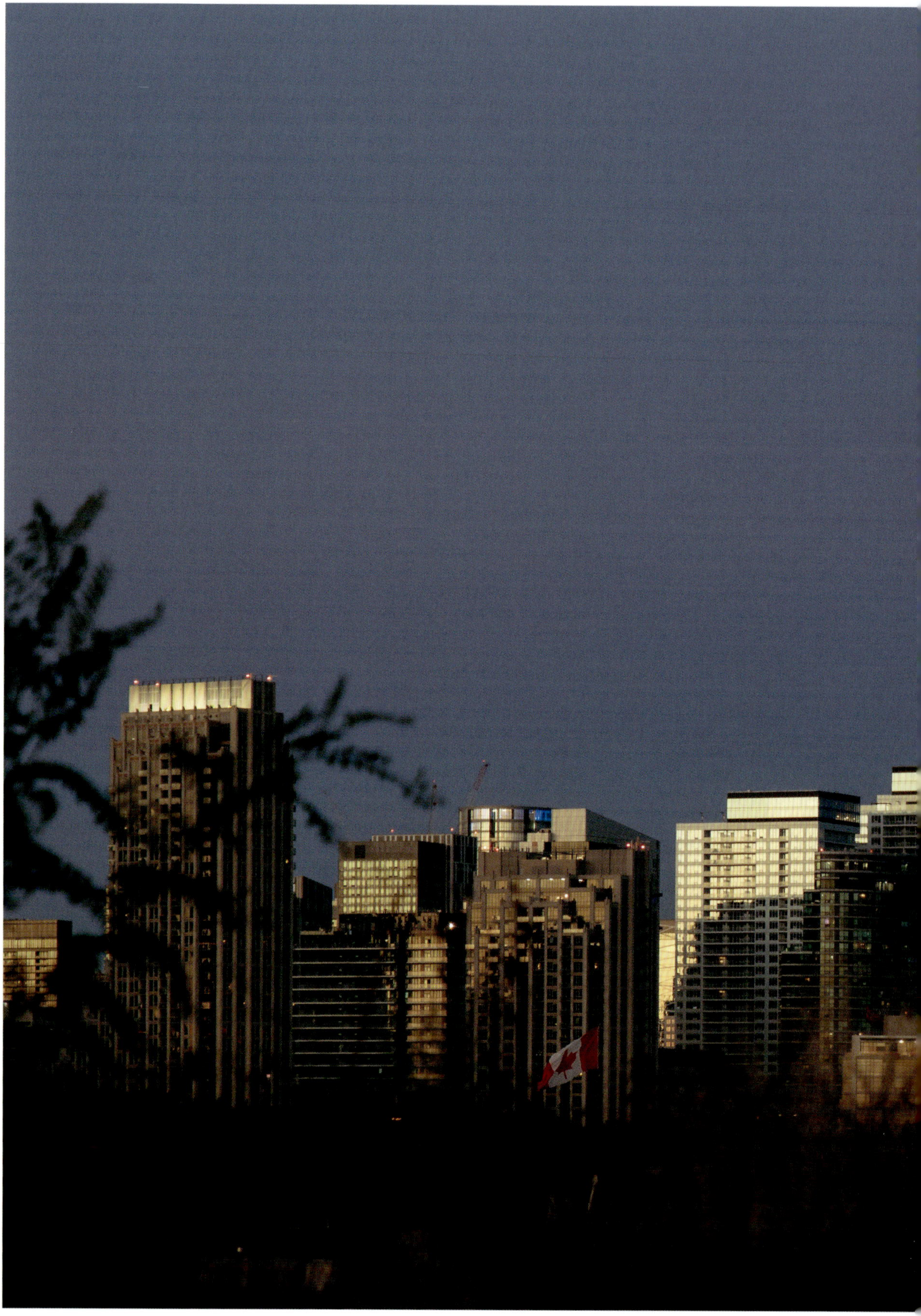

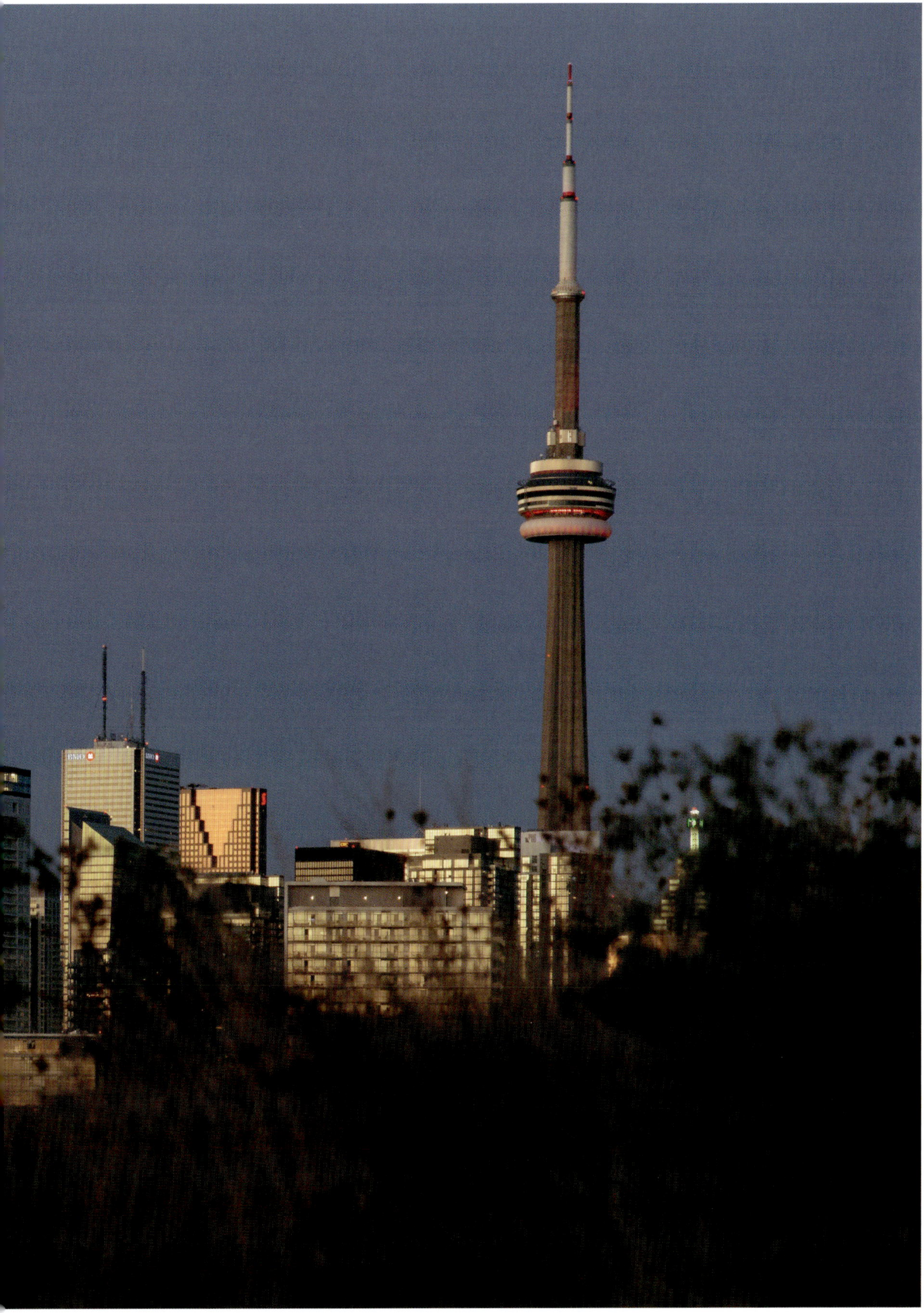

The following excerpts present the voices of three individuals, recorded at two distinct moments in time. These narratives explore the evolution of their reflections on Jewish identity and the impact of antisemitism, offering a raw, intimate glimpse into their personal journeys.

The first set of interviews was conducted in 2020/21. The second took place a few months after the October 7th terrorist attack by Hamas in 2023.

The Reflective Drifter (2021)

Navigating between different cultural worlds, they carry a steady awareness of their Jewish identity in environments where it goes unrecognized. Though distanced from religious practice, they remain deeply connected to their Jewish heritage, guided by a sense of responsibility to preserve it in an increasingly marginalized world.

I went to school with a Polish girl, and I remember she knew I was Jewish because we went to school together for years. And eventually it came out that my family came from Poland, and she said to me, "Well, that's so funny, I had no idea there were Polish Jews." I said, "Well, there actually used to be quite a few of them, and then there was a thing that happened." And she's like hard Polish—Polish is her first language, she was born there, she moved here—and it just didn't ever occur to her because it wasn't important to her, to pull the history that all the Jews got killed.

Usually a lot of people that I grew up with and went to school with can be like, "Oh, my parents or grandparents came from a different country" and most of them are like, "I identify as being Polish or Ukrainian." My family is Polish and Austrian, and I don't feel any connection to Polish or Austrian culture in the slightest, but I do feel a strong connection to Jewish culture through those same family members. You know, their nationality is not important to me, but their cultural identity has been important.

My relationship to Judaism is very interesting. I didn't grow up with any Jews. I went to camp, and all my Jewish friends are from camp, and I went to Hebrew Sunday school, but I went to public school in Toronto. Still, to this day most of my friends are not Jewish. I find that as I grow older and the less time I spend in Jewish spaces, the more Jewish I tend to be.

I'm a musician; I play in country bands. I spent a lot of time in the Prairies, and we toured through the States. I hang out with a lot of cowboys, and that's something that's a big part of my own identity. And the more I'm in those spaces, the more it makes me realize that I am Jewish, because I'm the only one there.

I never really experienced what I would call violent antisemitism, but there was definitely tons on the playground, like, "You Jewed me out of this." Or, like, jokes about Jews with big noses or, when I was a kid, jokes about the Holocaust were fine on the schoolyard. When I was a kid I never felt like anyone was violent towards me or thought less of me because I was Jewish. It was a far more casual antisemitism.

We are what I would call an invisible minority. It's still almost cool to be antisemitic, especially now in Trump's America. I know tons of people who I consider to be smart, forward-thinking, compassionate people, and then they get caught up in weird conspiracy theories. But, almost always, all of these conspiracy theories contain antisemitism. People are totally unafraid of going there, and I find it insane. People are like, "Black Lives Matter, but all the Jews should die," and that's still totally normal in spaces that are compassionate, humanist. You know, well-educated people still hate Jews, which is just insane to me.

I think, to me, one of the reasons that I feel Jewish, and that I want to continue being Jewish, is I see the erasure of Jews in the world. I know that's where my people come from, and I don't want that to be lost. I love a Friday-night dinner, but my partner, she's not Jewish. We don't light the candles for Hanukkah at home; we don't light the Shabbat candles every Friday night. The ritual of it doesn't really have any impact on my day-to-day life, but it's important to me that someone in my family is organizing it because I think that it's important to continue doing that.

I would say the biggest shock for me was when there was the white-supremacist rally in Charlottesville a few years ago. And there were young dudes walking through the streets saying, "Jews will not replace us." And that, for me, was a huge wake-up call of like, holy shit, these people really want to kill Jews.

I find the more negative information that's out there, or the more negativity around Jews that happens, that makes me go "I'm Jewish" even more. For example, I'm a pretty goyish-passing Jew, and if I never said anything I could go through my entire life and nobody would ever know I was Jewish. But if something were to come up where people said, "Hey, we're going to start systematically killing all the Jews," I would be included on that list and they'd come for me, even though it [my Judaism] is not super important to me in a lot of ways. But when it comes to the people who are like, "We want to kill Jews," they'd include me on that list, which makes me become defensive about it. Like I said, I think the more persecution that is happening towards Jews, the more Jewish I feel, and I think part of that's a little bit of a don't-fuck-with-me attitude.

And in a lot of cases, if I felt comfortable and I had been drinking with them [people] for a little while, I'd be like, "I'm Jewish," and see what kind of stuff comes back. And oftentimes it's curiosity, which comes from, I think, not a bad place at all. Even if there's some ignorance that might go along with that, I think, whatever, if I can help educate these people, that's okay. But sometimes you just suss it out and are like, "Oh, you know what, I feel like it might be inviting trouble to say I'm Jewish.

It might not be, but why bring it up." I find that more often people will ask me if I'm Jewish because I'll let something slip, some little bit of Yiddish, or, I don't know, I'll say something and people don't know what I'm talking about.

I don't want to talk about it, because I see both sides of it so clearly. And if I'm talking to Jews about it, then I'll end up taking the other side and then it becomes an argument. And if I'm talking to non-Jews about it, I'll take the Jewish side. And then that becomes an argument. It seems to me that nobody really wants to listen to what anybody else has to say about it. Everyone just wants to say their opinions on it, and I don't find that's constructive. I'm not going to solve the problem by talking it over with some pals; all that's going to happen is we're all going to get upset and everyone's going to make assumptions about the other people based on that conversation. I don't like to talk about.

The Reflective Drifter (February 2024)

Navigating between different cultural worlds, they carry a steady awareness of their Jewish identity in environments where it goes unrecognized. Though distanced from religious practice, they remain deeply connected to their Jewish heritage, guided by a sense of responsibility to preserve it in an increasingly marginalized world.

I can't speak for everyone, obviously, but I think most Jews, and certainly almost everyone that I know, felt a collective trauma response. When I got the news I felt horrified, felt terrified, and you know what, I've never felt more Jewish in my life. I've never felt more strongly about my identity, about my people, about our safety.

I will say that my initial reaction and how I feel about it now are drastically different. Over the last few months, I had to have a lot of hard conversations, and I had to do a lot of reading, and talk to other people with different experiences than mine, or even some people who have very similar experiences to mine, to try to get a bigger view on the whole thing.

And now I'm still upset about the seeming hopelessness of it all. And I'm mortified by the violence that I see. My initial thought was, Oh my God they're coming to get us again. I think there's a lot of antisemitism in the world and I also think there's confusion for a lot of people between antisemitism and anti-Zionism. I think that a lot of people are really angry, justifiably so, and I'm really terrified of the sort of lack of nuance around the conversation and how it has really become a stark sort of black and white. Especially for a lot of the people that I am in circles with—young leftist people. The scariest thing to me is, I mean obviously other than the deplorable violence and murder, the scariest thing that I'm personally experiencing is just people not being able to talk to each other about it.

Right after October 7th, for the first few weeks I felt a responsibility to go on Instagram, to go on my social media and speak up for Jews. Because I saw in my circle a lot of people weren't doing that. And a lot of people were just jumping on to say a bunch of stuff and I was just like, hey, can we take a second to maybe consider, you know, the whole picture and how other people might feel? And I had a lot of really hard conversations. I've had some conversations with people that were incredibly healing. And even if we disagreed, it just reaffirmed our shared humanity, which I think is really important right now. But I also have had some conversations with people where I was like, okay, I might not have the same relationship with that person ever again. I really spent the first three weeks just feeling my trauma response and taking no time to reflect on that.

At the beginning of all of this, when I saw people chanting—friends of mine chanting "Globalize the Intifada"—I was like, these people wanna kill me, these people want me dead. Seeing people wave signs [that said] "From the River to the Sea" and all this stuff that I was always taught was antisemitic, either overtly or antisemitic dog whistles. But I have sort of come to believe that 90% of the people who are walking in these protests saying "Intifada, Intifada" mean it simply to say, shrug off oppression and have Palestine be free. I really don't think that most of those people understand that the Intifada was an actual thing that happened in Israel—the suicide bombings and the collective trauma that exists around that for Jews the world over. I think a lot of people are swept up in a tide; they feel very strongly that there is something wrong happening there. I think it's pretty hard to look at what's happening and say there isn't, you know.

It's taken me quite a bit of time to try to intellectually remove myself from some of that stuff that's happening and say, yes, there's tons of antisemitism. I'm really scared of people's inability to separate Jews from Israel. I think there's, especially in the circles that I'm in, tons of conversation about how anti-Zionism is not antisemitism. I'm like, let's really try, if we're gonna be anti-Israel or critical of the government, to not be antisemitic. But the Israeli flag is a huge Star of

David, and 98% of the people on the planet aren't making that distinction. And so I think it is really terrible, and really terrifying. I am trying to be more optimistic and trying to be more understanding of people who are in those protests. Because I really do believe that the majority of people who are involved in that movement are not coming from a place of antisemitism or of hatred. And even if they're using language that we think is violent towards Jews and antisemitic . . . I wish that they were more willing to hear us say that and go, "Okay, let's try not to use that language," which I think they would do if it were other people that were involved in this. And I think that's a little bit of the scary side of antisemitism.

Ultimately it's not helpful to fight with any of them at all, which I tried to do for a month. I tried to take that on. It made me miserable. It made me feel terrible to yell against, you know, a sea of people all disagreeing with me. I think a lot of young people in North America view everything through a Western settler/colonial lens, which is really hard to apply to a piece of land that's been fought over for thousands and thousands of years and changed hands a bunch of times.

I was shocked at how affected I was by this. I would say, and I'm sure what I'm about to say comes from a place of immense privilege, but I wasn't thinking about Israel all that much until this happened. I think one of the crazy things that happened after October 7th is that all of a sudden every Jew was forced into a conversation, and forced to have an opinion, on something that we weren't necessarily ready for. And all of that in the midst of also going through this trauma response and needing to talk about it.

I'm talking about being able to hold two things at once. It took me time and needing to do some research, and some hard conversations and hard realizations about myself. And I think that for these other people who are ripping down [hostage] posters, they feel like they are morally right. And they're in this gigantic group—it's clear that that is the group that has the loudest voice—and I think that that gives them a little bit of armor. I felt like I had to do more research; I had to find some humanity to hold. Because I wouldn't be able to talk to people otherwise. And I think that for a lot of those people, they don't feel the need to do that deep dive, or have those hard conversations, because they think they're right already.

I feel proudly and strongly Jewish. I feel there has been a shift. Maybe it wasn't a shift; maybe I've just become more aware of the way that the world thinks of Jews. But I feel any change that I have had is an external thing where I think my views on myself as a Jew, what that means to me, how I exist in that community, I don't really think that has changed. But I do notice now that the world, I think, thinks of Jews differently. Or maybe thinks of them in the same way they always did, and I wasn't clocking that before.

I've been incredibly thankful for other Jews in my life who are making space to have these conversations. For the last few months there's been a weekly Zoom that's like a "feelings circle" for young Western leftist Jews, to talk about how it makes us feel to have these difficult conversations with our friends, or with our families, to disagree with people and to agree with people. It's been an incredible space just for sharing.

I think, hopefully, over the next little while we'll all be able to talk about it. I think we're going to be talking about it for a long time. I think it's going to be really hard for Jews for it to just fade away. I do think for a lot of people it is a "conflict of the year." Given some time, most people won't be thinking about it all that much. But I think it's gonna stay with us.

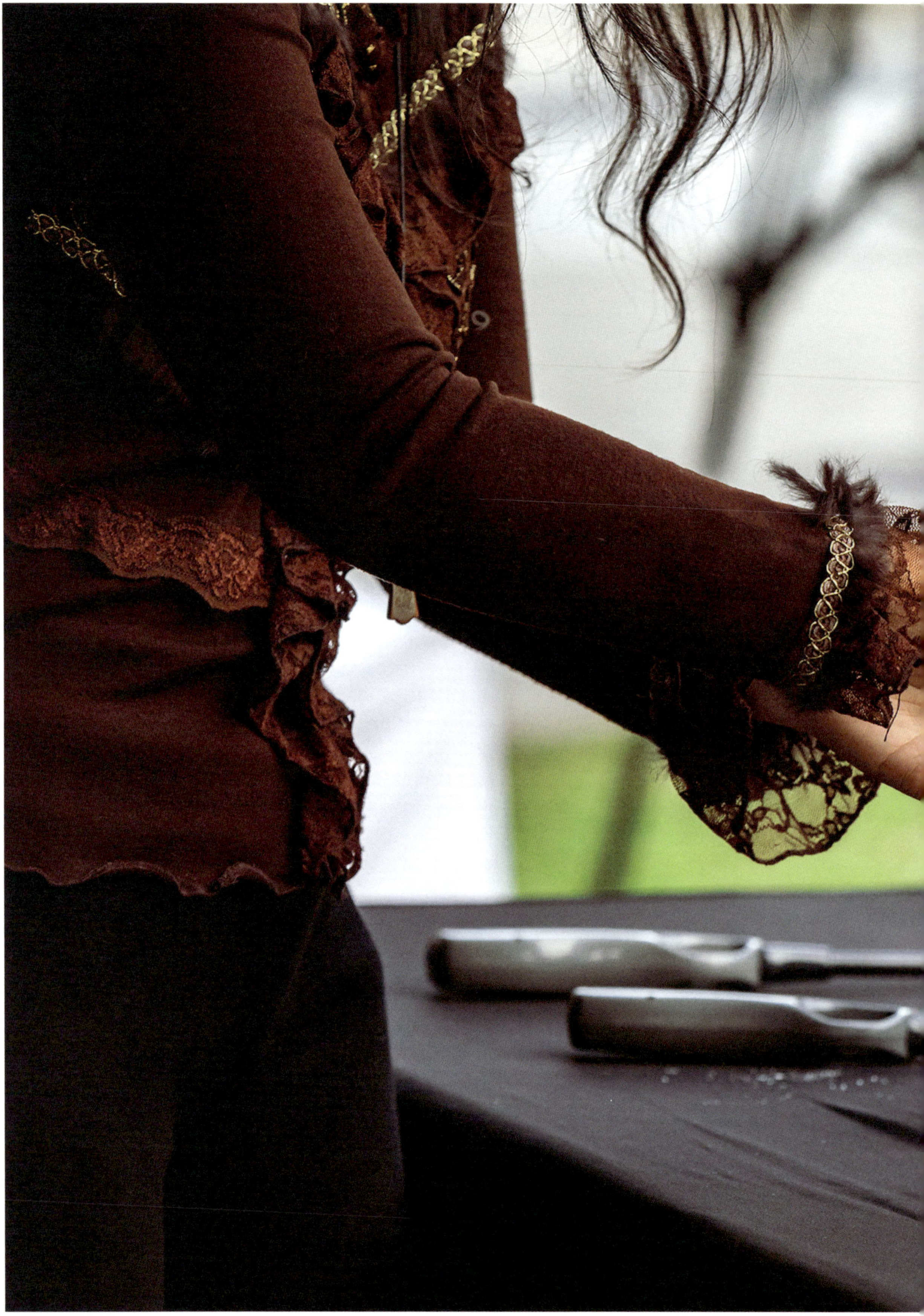

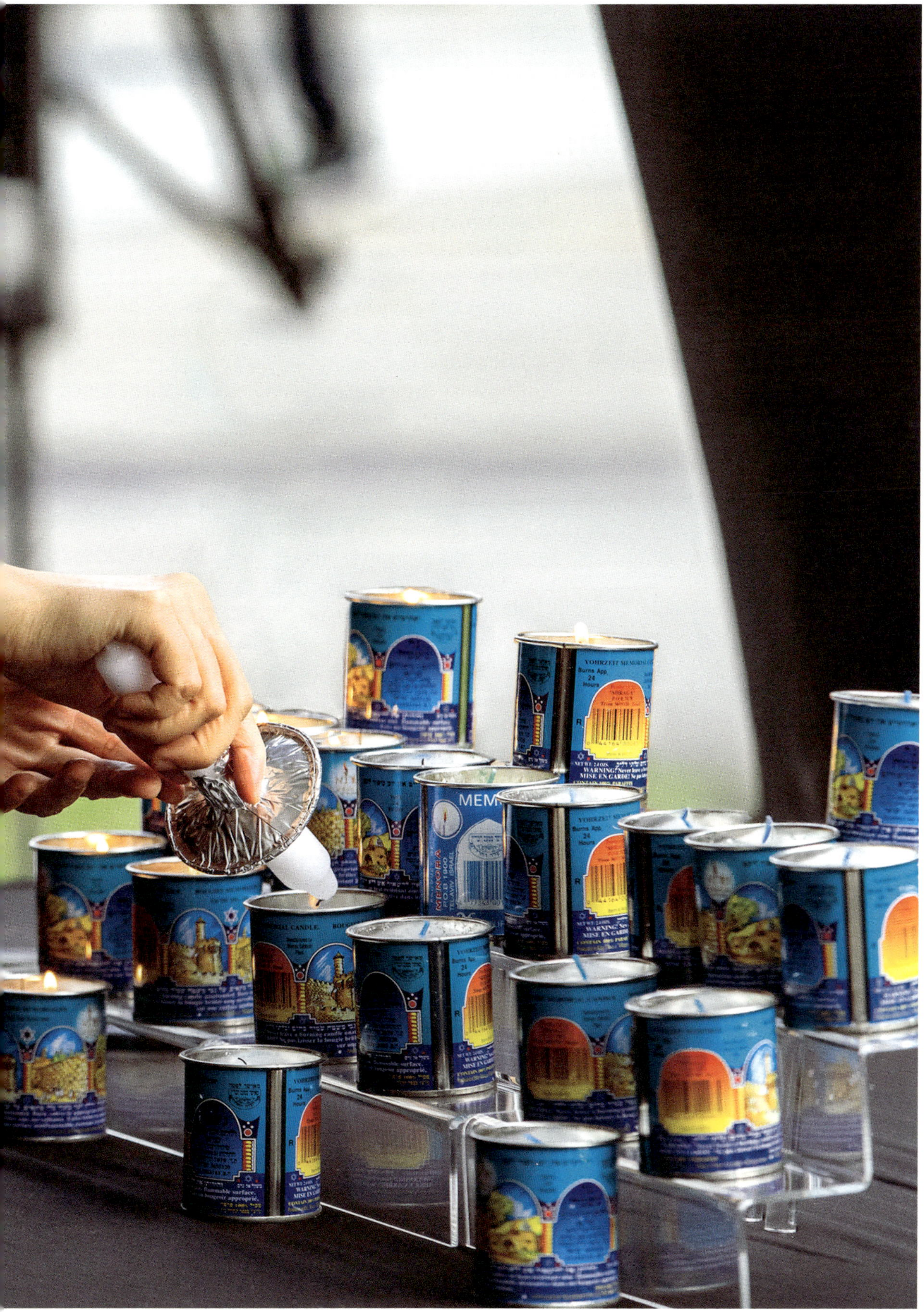
MEM
MEMORIA
P.O.B 1900
Burns App.
24
Hours
WARNING!
MISE EN GARDE!

The Principled Dissenter (2020)

Carrying a deep historical awareness, they balance the weight of the past with their personal identity, mindful of the intricate forces that shape both. In today's challenging world, they offer a perspective on the navigation of dissent.

I recognize that there's probably no two Jews in the world who will agree on what it means to be Jewish. It's meant different things at different times in my life, that's for sure. I had a pretty religious upbringing; I went to Hebrew school weeknights and Sunday mornings. My father changed his name when he came to Canada in order for it not to sound too Jewish. They [my family] had a great deal of ambivalence about being Jewish, and therefore, so do I. We were as Jews at once better than everybody else and worse than everybody else, and so it was a constant source of pride and shame. I think that's why one has perhaps to be a little bit careful or one has learned to be careful, whether it's necessary or not, about disclosing one's Jewishness.

What does it mean to be Jewish right now? It's about what I communicate to my four-year-old daughter about being Jewish. Since I moved out of my parents' house, I never had Shabbat. Although I moved in and out of Judaism in different ways throughout my adult life, I never did that [celebrated Shabbat] until after my daughter was born, at my partner's request, and my partner is not Jewish. So that's a big part of being Jewish now. Having an understanding of Torah has pretty much always been important for me in terms of what it means to be Jewish, that I can read Hebrew a little bit, that I've translated Torah in my work. What else does it mean to be Jewish to me? There's been barely a day in my life that some kind of understanding of the Holocaust has not occurred to me. It's been a huge factor in my life. So the Holocaust, having Shabbat, an understanding of Torah, and discussing Jewishness, and ways of practicing it or not with my immediate family, those are like touchstones for Judaism for me now.

I did a lot of reading about the history of the Holocaust and lived under a very dark cloud around it for several years. Right now it just feels like a deeply embedded cultural memory that I will never shake. My grandparents left Eastern Europe around the turn of the last century because they saw trouble, fled the pogroms of the czar, and went to England. I have a memory of being a child of, I don't know, maybe eight or ten years old, and lying on the living room floor in front of my parents facing the TV so they couldn't see my face. Something awful about the Holocaust came on. Upon the liberation of the camps there were bulldozers that were pushing bodies into mass graves. And I saw that, and my father said, "Change the channel; don't let Simon see that." And my mother said, "No, let him see what those bastards did." And I think that it still affects me.

In my childhood and through my adolescence, I guess there were occasions, not that many, but there were occasions when I was called a "fucking Jew," and that hurts. I'd say even into my adult and professional life there has been the occasional microaggression; nothing major (if you can say that about a microaggression), but it's never nothing, right? Every time I hear news about antisemitism I'm surprised by it. I guess I shouldn't be.

I recently visited Prince Edward County for a few days, and when we thought about the possibility of moving there I started doing a little bit of googling and found that there have been recent instances of antisemitism and it made me . . . it was very unpleasant to discover. It's quite a white part of the province and that makes us uncomfortable, just the very whiteness of it. And that the antisemitism was something that had occurred to a young girl, a high school student. I don't think it means that Jews need to stick together. There'd be no point in fighting antisemitism strictly in the Jewish community. It's likely not coming from there, right? I think we need to fight antisemitism along with antiracism, homophobia, and antitrans actions. I think we need to fight all of that. They're all different but related things; we need to fight all of them.

I think it might be fair to say that Jews are in some aspect very chameleonic; we've adapted to every culture that we've lived in. In every culture we've lived in for 2,000 years, we have also kept the community together through ritual. And I have to say, above all Torah, because even today I can go anywhere in the world, and I could have done so at any time in history, and no matter what Jewish culture I belonged to, I could identify with Jews anywhere in the world through Torah. And so that is what every Jew, whether they know it or not, has in common with every other Jew that has ever existed.

I recognize that a lot of anti-Zionism is in fact rooted in antisemitism. And I consider that really unfortunate. You could say, well, there's a good reason to be anti-Zionist, but that's not the reason why a lot of people are anti-Zionist. They are often anti-Zionist because they have been tinged one way or another by antisemitism. It's the reason why I stopped going to demonstrations against the state of Israel, because I found that those demonstrations attracted not just anti-Zionists but antisemites, and I stopped going.

We like to dine outside often, and we have a teeny little backyard right beside our neighbor's backyard. And so on Shabbat occasionally, because the weather has been nice, we'll eat outside, and I'm accustomed throughout the Shabbat meal to keep my kippah on. But there have been a couple times when I took it off because I felt uncomfortable about the neighbors seeing it. It's awful, but it's true. So that's one space where it's happened recently, and for sure there have been others where I've downplayed my Jewishness. I mean, it often just doesn't come up. I'm sure that there have been other occasions; it doesn't have to come up and I can downplay it. I can pass; we can pass.

The Principled Dissenter (Febuary 2024)

Carrying a deep historical awareness, they balance the weight of the past with their personal identity, mindful of the intricate forces that shape both. In today's challenging world, they offer a perspective on the navigation of dissent.

I understood the need for security when October 7th happened. Like everybody, I was mortified at the loss of lives. I don't think that indiscriminate murder and rape are at all appropriate responses to oppression. And so I was stunned by the attack and was apprehensive about what was going to happen next. And my fears were more than proven when Israel and Netanyahu responded the way they did. You know, following October 7th I was on the border of a nervous breakdown because of those events.

I've been to quite a few demonstrations in support of the Palestinians. I'm a member of the Jewish Faculty Network that is opposed to genocide, that is opposed to discrimination against Arabs and Palestinians. If you're asking about my response after October 7th, I could tell you I responded profoundly. It ruined a semester for me. What's happening in Gaza is not being done in my name. I refuse to associate with it. In fact, I have demonstrated against it on quite a few occasions. Furthermore, because where I work a lot of people know that I'm Jewish, I wear a keffiyeh. It's important to me that people know that being a Jew doesn't make me a Zionist. And let's be clear, I'm a Jew. I have not renounced my Judaism.

Years ago, I attended anti-Zionist demonstrations in front of the Israeli consulate when it was in the neighborhood on Bloor Street near University Avenue. I went to a couple of those demonstrations and stopped going because I felt the presence of antisemitism. In the more recent demonstrations, that is, since October 7th, I've not experienced a speck of antisemitism. My only discomfort in being in those demonstrations is that I can't believe I have to do this. As a Jew I can't believe that I have to demonstrate against the Israeli government. To me it's a horror, but here we are.

I'm distinctly Jewish. I consider myself a secular Jew. I have a seven-year-old daughter and we make Shabbat every Friday night. We want to give her a sense of being Jewish. She identifies as Jewish, though my partner is not. I continue to hold Torah in high esteem. My Jewishness has changed as of October 7th; I relate to it differently. I don't think you can interview me about my Jewishness and my responses to antisemitism post–October 7th without discussing my views on Zionism.

It's also my understanding that acts of antisemitism are on the rise. And to me, that's a sign that what's happening in Gaza does not do anything to improve the security of Jews. Quite the contrary—this is making things more dangerous for us. Because people don't know the difference between Judaism and Zionism, people need to be educated. I think the rise of fascism in the United States has a lot to do with white supremacy. I think the polarization in the United States and elsewhere between left and right has a lot to do with it. I mean, in a lot of ways it's the same old story. People are afraid of Jews.

I hate to see the polarization that's happening in the Jewish community. This is not to anyone's benefit. If today someone doesn't recognize that there is a breadth of positions in Judaism or any community, you know, something's not working. Someone reminded me recently of a cartoon about a [well-known] joke: A Jew is shipwrecked, and he's abandoned on a deserted island. Years later when they come to rescue him they see he's built two shuls, and they say, "You're one person on a desert island, why do you need two shuls? One I could understand." And he goes, "That shul, I go to. That one, if you paid me a million dollars I wouldn't go!"

I seldom look at the comments [on social media] because I find a lot of the comments on all sides of the spectrum to be often uninformed and poorly articulated, and it's frustrating to even look at them. So I seldom look at people's comments, and I never make any, never. I don't comment, because I'm not going to engage in debate in that way; it's not productive. And I fear being in an echo chamber.

You know, I had a fear of being Jewish publicly that came from my parents, who did live through the years of the Holocaust, and I inherited a certain amount of that. But I'm happy to say that I no longer take my kippah off. I'm far more comfortable now. For some reason, and it's not that easy to explain, but I no longer feel that way. I guess I'm just older. I've gotten over a lot of that, and I've shed a lot of fears about what other people may think. So yeah, I keep it on now.

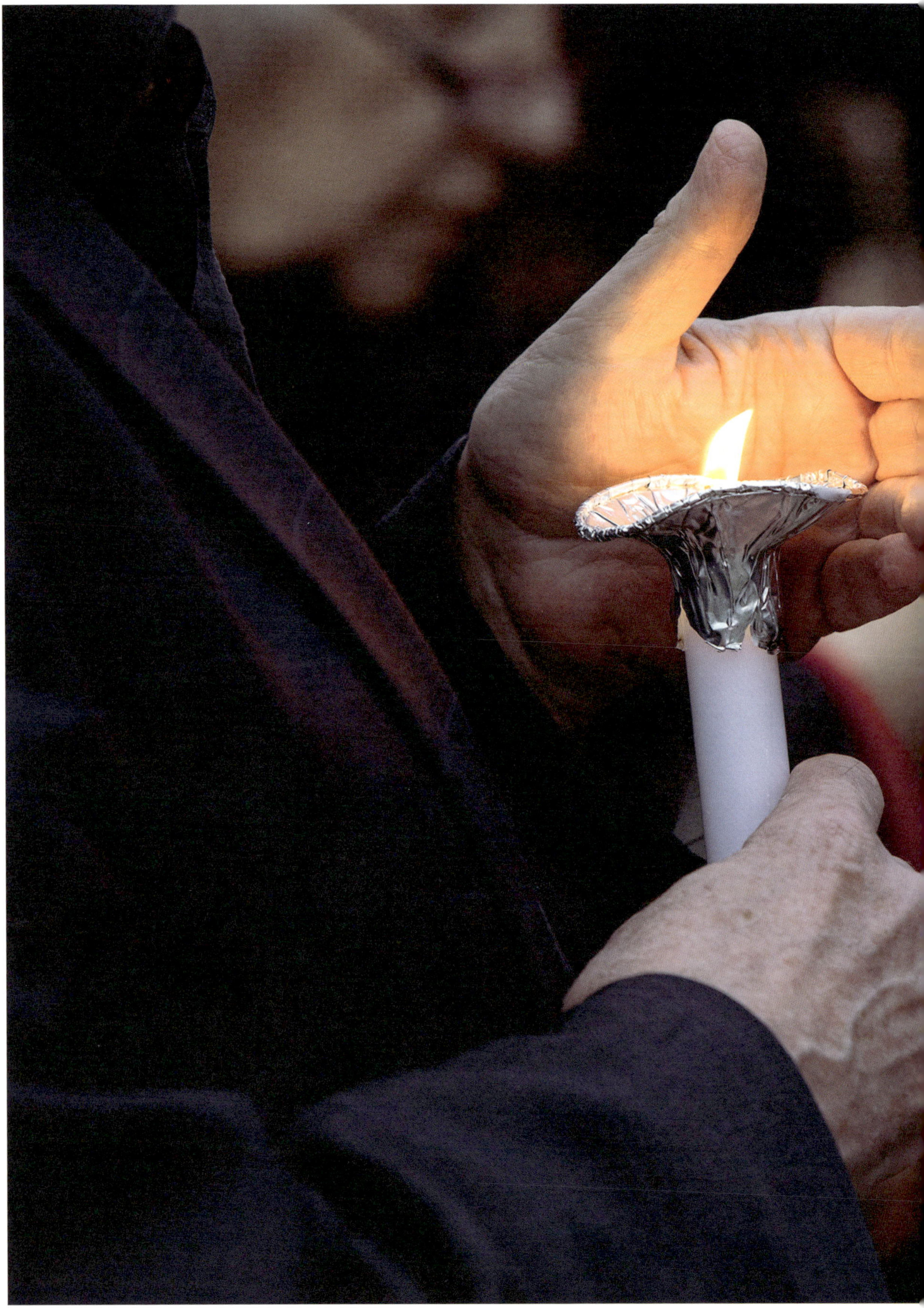

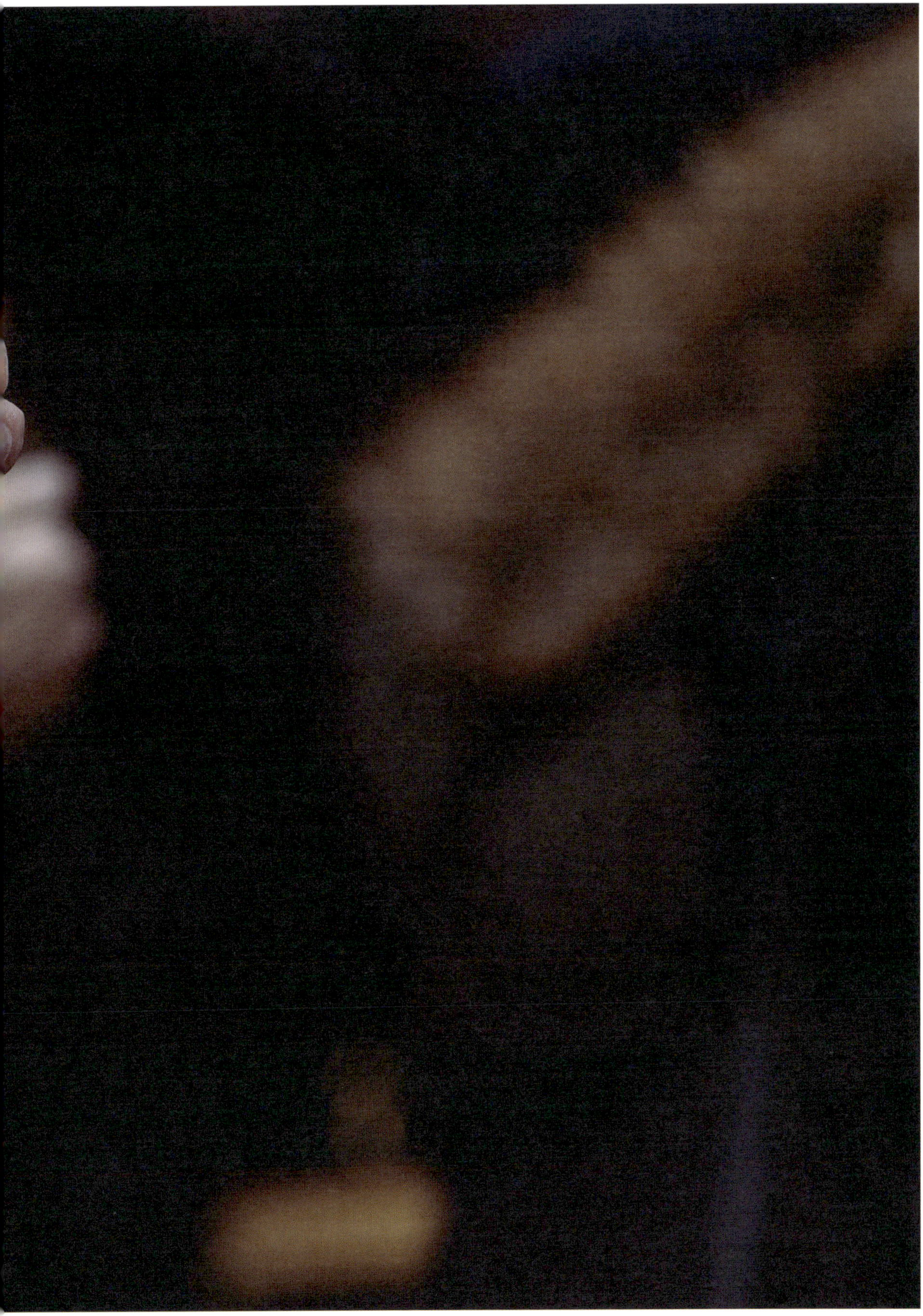

The Informed Realist (2020)

Guided by a deep understanding of how history, politics, and personal identity intersect, they meet the world's complexities with clear-eyed pragmatism. Steadfast and resolute, they are committed to protecting and preserving both their community and their identity.

My identification as a Jew is partly from a religious perspective, but more so from a cultural and tradition perspective. For me it is a way of being in the world that identifies with the people in my past, family members, friends, and the traditions that were passed down. It's not, for me, about things that are identified in the religious canon of the five books and the Mishnah and the Torah and all of that, because that's not how I identify myself. It's more from how, culturally, my people lived in life and how those traditions got passed from generation to generation. And now from me to my next generation, my children.

I identify myself as a Canadian for sure, but my primary [identity] would be Jewish. I wear a Star of David around my neck and I'm proud of it. I'm not going to hide who I am as a Jew because I don't think that anybody should have to hide who they are, what they practice, or how they believe. We've come too far for that. It's not fifty or seventy years ago, it's 2020, and people should be proud of whatever their heritage is and they shouldn't feel that they have to hide it in any way.

I think it [Jewish geography] exists in other cultures where people are one or two or five degrees removed from somebody in their cultural or in their religious group. It seems to be significant with Jews because Jews were excluded from so much. So it forced them to be closer and have a greater bond and togetherness because they were all in it themselves. Not against everybody else, but everybody seemed to be against them. The only thing they could do as Jews was to bind themselves together. That meant closer connections between themselves, whether it was friendship level, business level, or educational level, and self-help societies where they tried to help each other out. This was a significant reason, I think, for why Jews were able to succeed in the face of all the adversity, because they had their own community, bound up together to make themselves better.

I find the rise of antisemitism threatening as a Jew, even in North America where our rights are enshrined, and it's a liberal democracy with rights and freedoms that people have fought for all people to enjoy. But I do find it threatening because at the end of the day there are still groupings and it's still tribal. Our tribe is smaller and is at risk just as any smaller tribe is at risk. We've never been the majority anywhere outside of Israel. It strikes me that the phrase "we're strangers in a strange land" and that we're visitors is still relevant, even in the face of having all the rights that we believe we have. I unfortunately think discrimination exists. It's there; you can see it with graffiti, you can see it with statements, you can see it with written word, you can see it with videos. If you scroll down the comments on any website, on any article, you will find discriminatory statements from people who can hide behind the anonymity of making a comment on an internet chat, and it never goes away.

I have experienced discrimination as a Jew. In junior high school I remember getting called out for being a Jew. And I remember going to the bathroom, and I was washing my hands and there were three guys that were not Jewish that were making comments about me and my Jewish friends, and they were threatening comments. And I remember that I was surprised because I thought we were friends.

My kids are aware. My son played on a rep basketball team, and when they visited another school in a different part of the city pennies were thrown at them. When his friends were playing hockey on rep teams and they played in arenas in different parts of the city, they got called out for being Jewish—as if that was something that was okay to say to somebody. I don't know where that's coming from. I don't think it's coming from the school level; I think it must be coming from the home, and the kids pick that up. Or they see stuff on TV, or they just model behaviors they see. They think it's okay to point out how someone practices their faith, or what group they're from, or what the color of their skin is and make a comment to make somebody feel insecure about that—even though we're in 2020. You wouldn't think that would still be a discussion point, but it still is.

I don't think I've been in a situation where I refrain from discussing Israel, because I don't think that muzzling my opinions on something that's important to me is something I would want to do. There'd have to be a reason to do that, so if I'm not in physical risk, then aside from that if somebody doesn't like what I have to say, then that's fine. People fought wars so that we could have freedoms to express how we feel. And they don't have to like everything I say, and I don't have to like everything they say, but I need to be able to have that opportunity to say it.

I think today's antisemitism is more insidious. It can't be actioned in the same way because too much has gone on in the past to allow for violence to take place. It can take the form of many different things, but it's not going to take the form of people hitting the streets and forcing Jews to, you know, clean the streets with toothbrushes. And it's not going to take the form of another Kristallnacht, but it can be a smaller version and still dangerous.

The Informed Realist (March 2024)

Guided by a deep understanding of how history, politics, and personal identity intersect, they meet the world's complexities with clear-eyed pragmatism. Steadfast and resolute, they are committed to protecting and preserving both their community and their identity.

I would say immediately after [October 7th] it just felt like this was a terrible war crime—a crime against humanity, a crime of human being against human being. But it was sort of peppered with an understanding that it was [only] going to be a matter of days, because of historical context, that you were going to have the support of the world about this tragedy and then it was going to turn. And it was inevitable. I remember talking about it, I remember thinking about it, and then it happened. So it was sadness of the event and then sadness of the predictability of the aftermath. I had some of my non-Jewish friends reach out within a week or so, and then I had a lot of people who I thought were connected to me on a certain level who did not respond, and it was disappointing.

I think every Jew I know, for the first little bit, couldn't sleep the way they used to. Waking up in the middle of the night, checking your phone, trying to understand what's going on. "Are there new events that I need to be aware of? Are there people I know that are at risk?" I think they refer to this as—what is that called when it's baked into your collective DNA?—generational trauma. I feel like there is an awakening of generational trauma where people are tapped into the existence of generations before, of what they experienced, and now this is the newest iteration of an old iteration and it affects us because it's on our mind.

I sometimes say to my kids I feel terrible that previous generations would look and say, "We left you the keys to the car and where have you taken us?" We were at a point where we thought we were going to drive that car to an even better place. And while we were driving that car on the highway, all of a sudden we were at great risk. And it's not necessarily by actions we've taken; it's by the world around us having decided that we had been guests of humanity, and good humanity, for quite a while, and now the tide has turned.

I would say it's like listening to your grandparents, who told you that the thin veil of antisemitism was two scratches away from being revealed. You have a tragic event take place on October 7th and instead of the response being some empathy for the victims, it becomes a renewed prosecution of Jews who were the victims of this event, and now they've become somehow the source of it. When it happened it just was a painful awareness that our grandparents' generation, which warned us about this, which said it never goes away—and we wanted to believe that it would be different—that sadly they were right. And it's heartbreaking because we thought we had progressed so far from that kind of religious-based hatred or culture-based hatred, and yet we really haven't.

It definitely feels there's a level of rage, and as a citizen of the city I look at it and say, "Well, does this make me feel safe?" I'm not sure the police have the ability to stop what's going on, and I don't feel that the people in the city fully appreciate what the risk is going forward. I just feel like if the police feel they're handcuffed and can't respond to the sort of more violent protests, then it becomes normalized. We have a bunch of police trying to stand with arms crossed and present some form of deterrence. But it's not real deterrence if people are climbing on your hospitals, if people are storming around making other people feel unsafe where their community lives.

And I don't think the police have the ability to do anything, because I think the understanding of how far a group can push has changed. You have groups protesting in an area localized to Jews at Avenue and Wilson. Imagine the response if a bunch of pro-Israel protestors showed up in a Muslim area, say Brampton or Mississauga or Markham, and tried to make the local residents feel uncomfortable at their restaurants, in their homes, in their residential areas. I don't think the response would be the same. I think there'd be much more outrage. There's a level of acceptance in the city that it's okay to harass Jews; it's okay to make things difficult for Jews because they can take it, or they're used to it, or that's just how it works. We've done a disservice to our citizens if we condition them into thinking that that's okay, because it's not okay.

I mean, Mount Sinai Hospital, downtown Toronto, is a hospital that serves the needs of the entire community—irrespective of what your religion is, what your nationality is, where you're from, and what your beliefs are. It should be off-limits; it's not a place to protest. Does it make sense that you have police encampments in Jewish day schools like Bialik on Bathurst, and other schools up north in Richmond Hill? What city do we live in that you have to have police encampments in front of schools, or that you have to have armed guards and security in front of synagogues? You don't have that in front of churches; you don't have that in front of mosques. We're conditioned, and it's become normalized that we expect to see serious security, police security, armed guards in front of synagogues.

As soon as those hostage signs were circulated, I went around the city with my son and we put them up for two days. All we were doing was trying to raise awareness for the issue of the hostages, which is the starting point of this whole conflict. And as a human being in the world how can you not stand for releasing people who have been abducted? It's just a basic human understanding. To see people rip them off without context, without caring, just saying, "I don't want the face of this hostage to be made aware to people," it's like they're not acknowledging it's an issue and they're endorsing the fact that it's okay. If someone wants to do that, that's on them and nobody can re-educate them. You wouldn't do that for a lost dog or a lost cat, but you're going to take a "Free the Hostage" poster that addresses a ten-year-old who's been abducted? Those people are lost.

My perspective on being a Jew has changed. I feel I am a little more hardened in my approach and in my thought process because of the events that I'm seeing now. I thought the needle had moved, and it hasn't moved as far as I thought. There is a different level of treatment, a different level of rules, and a different level of response to events that take place affecting my community of Jews as opposed to how every other community in the world gets treated. It's disappointing and it's not justice and it's not fairness. The standard that is applied is uneven, the response to events is uneven, and it's disappointing. Our kids are watching and they're seeing how we respond. Are we responding in a way that we're making them proud? Or are we responding in a way that's a little bit milky and we're not really taking a stand? They're watching and, I think, in some ways changing their outlook.

It can be exhausting because sometimes you're just reinforcing how you feel. And it's frustrating because you feel like you're fighting against a tidal wave of lack of understanding, and you can't educate people about your idea because they don't want that. They're hardened on their views, and it's hard. And there's more of them than us, and that's why we're constantly fighting the fight of truth.

I was very sad about the response in North America, the response from the UN, and the silence of the UN Women's groups. And women's groups across the United States that previously had a stance on sexual violence but had a completely different response to what was going on in Israel. What, we're not supposed to believe them until we have more irrefutable evidence? "Where are the rape kits? Where are the testimonies?" I thought the whole point was we're supposed to believe the victim absent from any information to the contrary. We have GoPro video from the perpetrators of these crimes. That's not enough.

Our victims have to suffer, and our victims have to be questioned, but everybody else in the world gets accepted at face value for whatever it is that they want to say. The saddest answer is a complete dehumanization of the Jewish experience, which is just something that's centuries old that we don't want to believe exists. But why else? What other explanation can there be that Jewish victims of rape have accountability questions and no other victims of rape do? How is it that the Jewish victims of hostage taking elicit no empathy, but when Boko Haram took their victims in Africa it was a worldwide event?

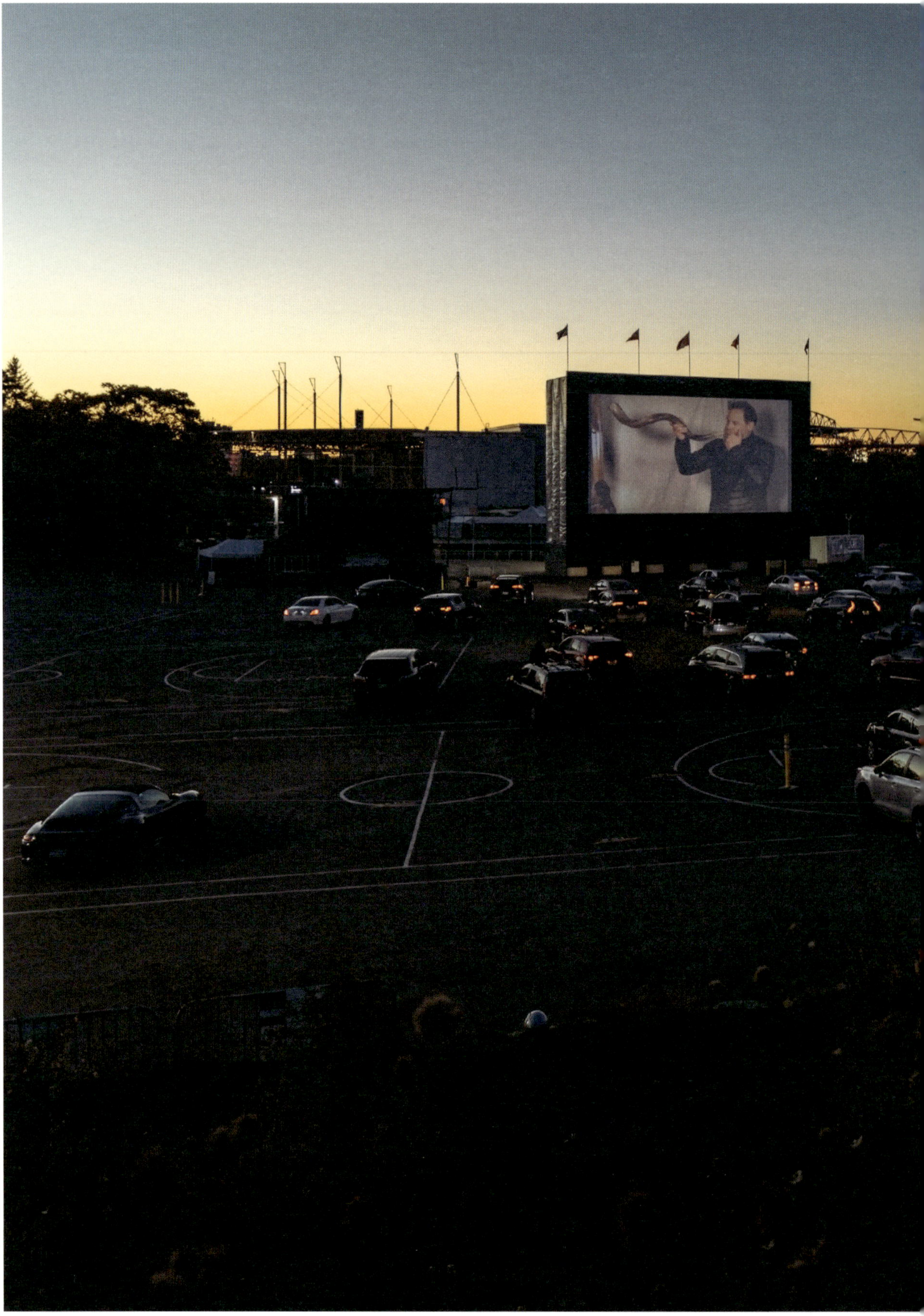

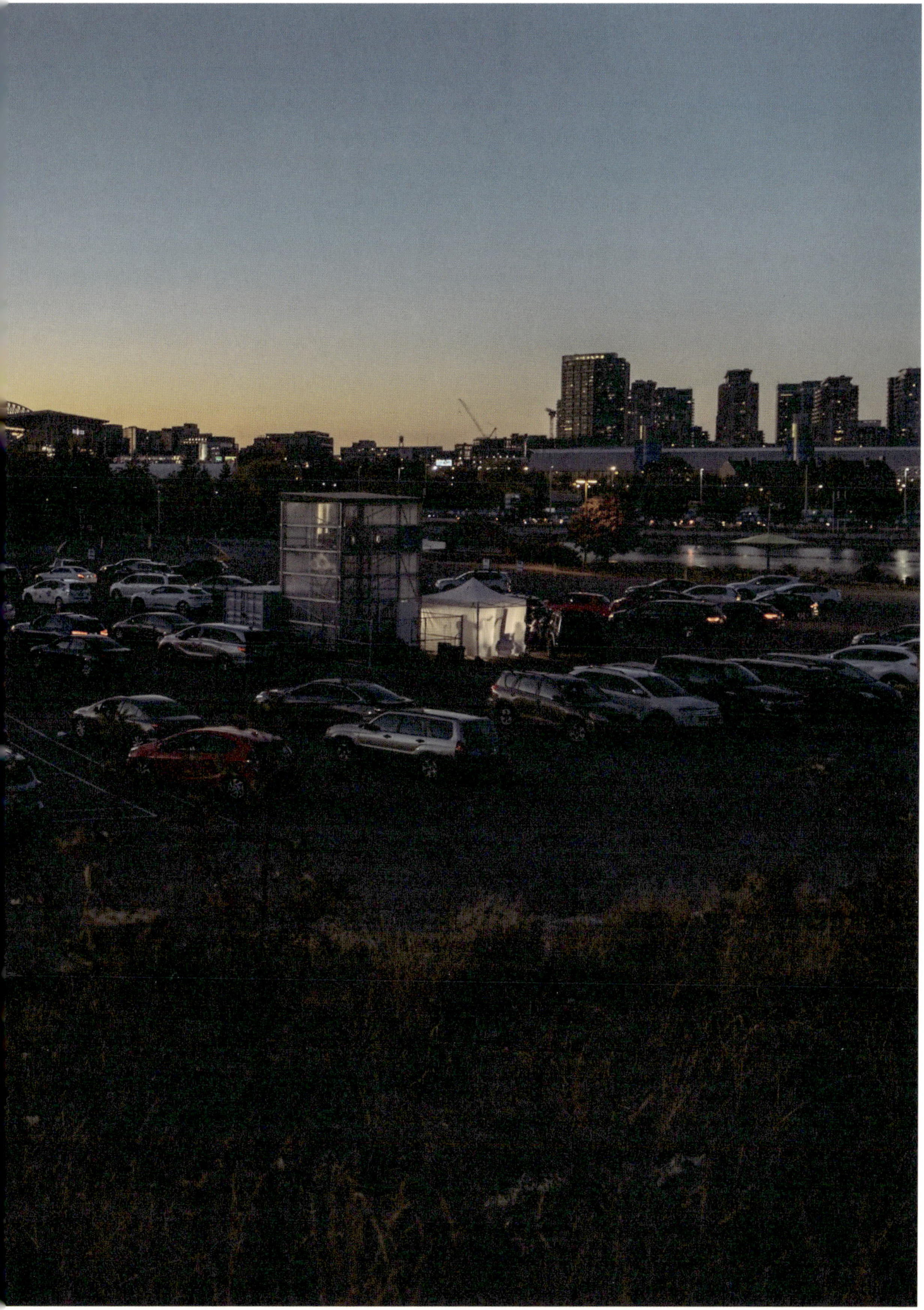

Kendell Pinkney is a Brooklyn-based playwright, arts and culture advocate, educator, and rabbi.

הושע נא! תלויה על בלימה. הושע נא!

Please save! It's hanging by a thread. Please save!
—Hoshanot from Hoshana Rabba

I am writing these words while suspended above the Midwest—my home of New York City nearly 1,000 kilometers behind me and Toronto several hundred kilometers over my right shoulder outside the airplane window. For a moment, all looks right with the world. I see a pretty muddle of blue sky dappled with downy clouds, suburbs and pastureland inching toward the gentle curve of the earth winking in the distance. It is a beautiful view. And in a moment, I feel it . . .

A rupture
A realization
A reckoning
Turbulence.

And I remember that I am a nervous flyer. It matters little that my logical brain can recount how statistically safe I am. In such moments I experience an electric hypervigilance; I am suspended between heaven and earth, held yet uncertain. The destabilizing force of feeling safe in one moment and then feeling your precarity in the next is bewildering. And strained as the flying metaphor may be, the overwhelming sense of bewilderment begins to touch the emotional terrain held in these pages. This is a book that moves between groundedness and unsettlement through its layering of images, fragments, and anonymous voices, shaping a form that mirrors the complexity of Jewish life today.

I am moved by the vulnerability represented in these pages. Many stories reflect my own experience, and there are just as many that do not.

Some perspectives align with my own, and others sit in great tension with my own. Regardless of where each story, interview, or photograph lands along that spectrum of alignment or alienation, one thing is clear: these are the perspectives of *ammi*, my people. All of them.

This work is not that of a single voice but a chorus of many. Divergent experiences and memories sing in counterpoint with one another, allowing the contradictions to shimmer and breathe, each part holding its place in the arrangement without overwhelming the rest. Moreover, this book invites us into profoundly liminal experiences and asks us to listen closely to the themes that emerge from within them: between past and present, visibility and erasure, personal testimony and public discourse.

In my pastoral work as a rabbi, I have felt just how deeply Jewish individuals, families, and communities across North-America have struggled to make sense of the world post-October 7th. Families talk past one another; friendships are torn apart over hastily posted social media missives; streams of op-eds deploy Talmudic analysis over a leader's or institution's absence (or preponderance) of statements trying to name suffering in a way that feels encompassing to all.

These are but a few examples. But when imagined at scale, the communal pain becomes unmistakable. Round and round we go circling the devastation of our hearts, questioning whether our families, communities, and the world can actually be repaired. It is all so dispiriting, so saddening, so overwhelming that I can finally sense the deep desperation underlying certain prayers that had heretofore only been rote texts:

G-d, please save . . .

Bring salvation . . .

G-d . . . save . . .

Without You there is no salvation . . .

please save . . .

man and beast . . .

G-d . . . please . . .

flesh and spirit and soul . . .

G-d, please save . . .

It's suspended on nothing . . .

It's hanging on by a thread . . . [1]

[1] These prayer fragments are drawn from the Hoshanah piyut (man and beast), attributed to the early poet Eleazer ben Kallir, who lived in the Land of Israel sometime in the sixth–seventh century CE.

And yet from within this feeling of desperation I remind myself that even if all feels hopeless, even if the Jewish people feel as if they are hanging on by a mere thread, that does not mean that a fall into the abyss is inevitable. Rather, it simply reflects what has always been the case: life, community, memory, love, history, nations, cultures, ideologies, ecologies, peoples, and every nearly riven thing under the sun is contingent—has *always* been hanging on by a thread. And once we accept that reality, unsettling as it may be, what is of greatest importance is how we choose to live in relation to that contingency.

This, to me, is the quiet power of *A Peoplehood | Amiut Yehudit.* It reminds us that art can create a space in which we are seen and see others, held and mirrored. The book carries us through belonging and community, cultural memory and its fractures, gestures of fortitude and of empowerment. It does not offer a single argument, nor does it seek to soothe us with certainty. Instead, it offers something else necessary to our moment: a practice of witnessing, of showing up to one another's truths, and of searching for steadiness in the in-between places.

The plane descends through thick clouds on an unseasonably rainy Los Angeles day. Whitecaps break in the bay below as we angle slowly toward the coast. My eyes are grateful for the sight of terra firma, but my heart skips as the wind skids the plane along its descent. Lower we go. The faster my heart beats. *G-d, please save . . .* I see the beach. The houses. I feel an updraft. *G-d, please . . .* I see cars, industrial buildings, rain. *G-d, please save . . .* I see the runway. The plane glides, hanging on by a thread. A final moment. *G-d please save . . . G-d please save . . . G-d please save . . . G-d please . . . G-d please . . . please.*

HISTORICAL PHOTOGRAPHS

Staszów community photographs, c. 1890s–1930s. Courtesy of the Rotenberg and Gottesman Families, and the Stashover-Slipia Congregation.

Berger family at Passover seder, Borden Street, Toronto, 1926. Ontario Jewish Archives (item 3786).

Family Passover seder, Toronto, 1990s. Photograph by Jeff Goode, Toronto Star / Getty Images.

ARCHIVAL EPHEMERA

Toronto Daily Star, June 22, 1937.

French Cleaners, 1938. Ontario Jewish Archives, Blankenstein Family Heritage Centre (fonds 17, series 5-3, file 65).

Employment rejection letter to Lillian Noble, Toronto, 1932. Philip Martin Collection, Ontario Jewish Archives, Blankenstein Family Heritage Centre (accession 2019-1-7).

Pierre Berton, "No Jews Need Apply," *Maclean's*, 1948. Courtesy of Maclean's.

"Jewry Must Perish" image with yellow Star of David and swastika, 2017. Courtesy of B'nai Brith Canada.

Image of high school exterior defaced with antisemitic graffiti, including a swastika and "Jews did 911," 2017. Courtesy of B'nai Brith Canada.

Image of guardrail on highway spray-painted with "Hitler was right," 2017. Courtesy of Friends of Simon Wiesenthal Center.

Screen grab from Vice News video of the Unite the Right rally, Charlottesville, 2017, showing white-nationalist demonstrators chanting "Jews will not replace us!"

Image of vandalized sign of Holocaust survivor Max Eisen, defaced with the German word "Achtung" ("warning"), 2018. Courtesy of UJA Federation of Greater Toronto.

Image of garage spray-painted with swastika and text "we watch" and "watch yourself," 2019. Courtesy of UJA Federation of Greater Toronto.

"Covid Caust" T-shirt, healthjusticetees.com, c. 2020.

Image of poster of Kfir Bibas, the youngest hostage kidnapped by Hamas, defaced with a swastika drawn on his forehead, 2024. Courtesy of Tamar Lyons.

Cartoon entitled *Yenta Theatre Presents Waiting for Godot*, by Roz Chast. The New Yorker Collection / The Cartoon Bank. © Condé Nast.

Cartoon with caption "First of all this conversation never happened." Paul Noth / CartoonStock.com.

SOCIAL MEDIA

@CIJAinfo, X, July 13, 2020. Courtesy of CIJA. Image from ctv.ca, © 2018 Sattalat Phukkum / Shutterstock.

@lindssoberano, X, July 13, 2020. Courtesy of Lindsay Soberano Wilson.

@BrooklynBen, X, July 13, 2020. Courtesy of Ben Austin.

@arielladan18, X, July 13, 2020. Courtesy of Ariella Daniels.

@stormb0401, X, July 13, 2020.

@randibergman, X, July 13, 2020. Courtesy of Randi Bergman.

@skjask, X, July 13, 2020. Courtesy of Shoshanna Keats Jaskoll.

@AshagerAraro, X, July 13, 2020.

@Byrun_nuryB, X, July 13, 2020.

@RyanAzr, X, July 13, 2020.

@michaelcoren, X, July 13, 2020.

@Ari_bacher, X, July 13, 2020. Courtesy of Ari Bacher.

@CombatASemitism, X, July 13, 2020. Courtesy of Combat Antisemitism Movement (CAM), statistics from B'nai Brith Canada Annual Audit of Antisemitic Incidents for 2019.

@Anthony_Koch, X, October 15, 2023. Photo by montreal-live.ca.

Image of police evacuating babies from Jewish daycare after threat, 2023. Canada United for Israel, X. Reposted with added text in the Facebook group "Everything Jewish Toronto" (anonymous).

@CanadianFSWC, X, April 19, 2024. Courtesy of Friends of Simon Wiesenthal Centre.

@moderntribe_jew, Instagram. Courtesy of Amy Becker. Cartoon by Erin Gillespie.

@moderntrib_jew, Instagram. Courtesy of Amy Becker. Illustration by Someecards.

@jewishgirlprobs, Instagram.

@moderntribe, Instagram. Courtesy of Amy Kritzer. Cartoon © Last Kiss, Inc., courtesy of John Lustig.

@bessbell and @SSCJoeDuenas, X. Image still from ABC News.

@hishersandoursofficial, Instagram.

DIGITAL MEDIA

Passover seder on Zoom, 2020. Courtesy of the Pulver family.

Email from Dani Etkin-Spigelman, Scout Logistics, 2014.

NEWSPAPER ARTICLES

Frederik Xavier-Duhamel, Alanna Smith, and Laura Stone, "Canadian Schools, Synagogues, Community Centres Ramp Up Security After Hamas Attack in Israel," *The Globe and Mail*, October 13, 2023.

Christopher Nardi, "Youth Arrested on Terror-Related Charges," *National Post*. Material republished with the express permission of National Post / Toronto Sun, a division of Postmedia Network Inc.

Marlo Glass, "Hate Crime Charges Laid After Doctor Harassed," *National Post*. Material republished with the express permission of National Post / Toronto Sun, a division of Postmedia Network Inc.

"Combating Holocaust Denial," *Toronto Star*, November 7, 2023. From the *Toronto Star*. © 2023 Toronto Star Newspapers Limited. All rights reserved. Used under license.

Marie Woolf, "Schools May Seek Legal Action for Anti-Semitism," *The Globe and Mail*, January 24, 2024.

Marie Woolf, "Former NDP Chief Says Jewish Members Feeling Uncomfortable in the Party," *The Globe and Mail*, March 8, 2024

Frederik Xavier-Duhamel, Mike Hager, and Lindsay Jones, "Jewish Communities Shaken by Spike in Hate Incidents Since Mideast War's Onset," *The Globe and Mail*, November 10, 2023. Photograph by Ryan Remiorz / The Canadian Press.

"If It's Not About Jews, Stop Targeting Them," Editorial, *Toronto Sun*, January 2, 2024. Material republished with the express permission of National Post / Toronto Sun, a division of Postmedia Network Inc.

Note

All third-party material is reproduced with permission of the rights holders to the best of abilities. Every effort has been made to identify and credit sources accurately.

ACKNOWLEDGMENTS

This book is the culmination of the generosity of many who accompanied me through its long evolution and whose belief made it possible.

This project was nurtured by the support of institutions and mentors who offered time, resources, and trust. I'm especially grateful to Katy McCormick and Toronto Metropolitan University's Documentary Media MFA program, where the work first took shape as an installation, and later at the Toronto Jewish Film Festival, where it was presented in film form.

I'm deeply thankful to those who, at different moments and stages, offered wisdom and insight, including Elizabeth Avedon, Alexa Becker, Olga Bondarenko, Neil Grunberg, Sara Lefton, and Sam Mogolinsky. A very special thank-you to Ruth Kaplan for her mentorship throughout all of the work's iterations.

I am indebted to the brilliant designer Caleb Cain Marcus of Luminosity Lab. His ability to listen, interpret, and elevate transformed this project, bringing shape and clarity to a vision I had long sought to realize.

To Michael Itkoff and the team at Daylight Books, thank you for your belief in the project and for shepherding it into the world with trust and care. I'm especially grateful to Ursula Damm for her steady guidance through production, and to Gabi Fastman for her thoughtful and nuanced copyediting.

I would like to express immeasurable appreciation to my interview participants who shared their thoughts with candor and generosity, breathing "life" into the work. The project would not have been possible without the vibrant Jewish community of Toronto, Canada.

I'm especially grateful for my family's love and constant support: my husband, Lorne, for his boundless enthusiasm and pride; my daughters, Charley and Sydney, for their words of encouragement; and my parents, Lynn and Gerry, for their wisdom and guidance. And finally, to Summer, whose constant companionship and love are deeply missed.

BIOGRAPHY

Marnie Salsky is a Toronto-based photographer and documentary media artist whose work explores Jewish identity, collective memory, and the lived experience of antisemitism. Through a conceptual documentary approach, she combines photographs, archival materials, interviews, and fragments of digital life to build layered narratives that extend the boundaries of traditional documentary practice.

She earned an MFA in documentary media from Toronto Metropolitan University. Her work spans installation, print, and film; an earlier iteration of this project was screened at the Toronto Jewish Film Festival.

Daylight

Publisher: Michael Itkoff
Creative Director: Ursula Damm
Copy Editor: Gabrielle Fastman

Creative Direction: Caleb Cain Marcus, Luminosity Lab

ISBN 978-1-954119-52-9
Printed by Ofset Yapimevi, Turkey

Daylight Books
E-mail: info@daylightbooks.org
Web: www.daylightbooks.org